THE
DISASTER-READY HOME

— A —
Step-by-Step
Emergency
Preparedness
Manual for
Sheltering
in Place

THE DISASTER-READY HOME

A Step-by-Step Emergency Preparedness Manual for Sheltering in Place

Creek Stewart, Author of *Survival Hacks*

ADAMS MEDIA

NEW YORK   LONDON   TORONTO   SYDNEY   NEW DELHI

Adams Media
An Imprint of Simon & Schuster, Inc.
100 Technology Center Drive
Stoughton, Massachusetts 02072

First Adams Media trade paperback edition January 2022

For information about special discounts for bulk purchases, please contact Simon & Schuster Special Sales at 1-866-506-1949 or business@simonandschuster.com.

The Simon & Schuster Speakers Bureau can bring authors to your live event. For more information or to book an event contact the Simon & Schuster Speakers Bureau at 1-866-248-3049 or visit our website at www.simonspeakers.com.

Interior design by Colleen Cunningham
Photographs by Creek Stewart

Manufactured in the United States of America

10 9 8 7 6   5 4

Library of Congress Cataloging-in-Publication Data has been applied for.

ISBN 978-1-5072-1736-8
ISBN 978-1-5072-1737-5 (ebook)

Contents

CHAPTER 5: SURVIVAL SPROUTING / 83

Part 2: Water / 95

CHAPTER 6: LONG-TERM WATER STORAGE / 97

CHAPTER 7: WATER STORAGE CONTAINERS / 107

CHAPTER 8: RENEWABLE WATER SOURCES / 125

Introduction

From hurricanes and tornadoes to ice storms and issues with compromised municipal water supplies, we've seen numerous recent disasters—both natural and manmade—cut off electrical or water service to hundreds of thousands of people, sometimes for weeks at a time. If a situation occurs that forces you to shelter in place at home, do you have everything you need to get you and your family through an undetermined period of time?

Before the COVID-19 pandemic, it was easy to write off this type of question as hypothetical thinking. But we now know that shelter-in-place situations can be a reality in our lives. The need to be prepared has never been more evident, and that is what *The Disaster-Ready Home* will help you do.

Food, water, shelter, heat, toilets, cooking—these are the essentials for daily life. This book will help you create and implement a system that allows you to meet each of these needs should a long-term shelter-in-place situation arise.

You'll find realistic solutions to help you do the following:

- Build a functional long-term food storage pantry that works with your diet, budget, and lifestyle
- Be prepared to cook food and boil water without using your traditional grid-tied kitchen appliances
- Set up long-term water storage (and renewable water sources)
- Establish an alternative heating solution if you live in a four-season environment
- Implement an off-grid toilet and human waste removal/storage system
- And more

This is not a book about how to go off grid, how to grow all your own food, how to move to the mountains, or how to homestead. I don't think any of these are practical preparedness solutions for the average suburban household in modern America. Instead, you'll find a realistic, achievable, affordable, and effective preparedness plan that I call the Disaster-Ready Home Plan. I've taken exactly what I've done in my own home, for my own family, and turned it into a step-by-step manual for you to follow to be better prepared to shelter in place inside your own home, wherever that might be.

This information is designed to help you build the buffer you've been looking for to get you and your family through uncertain times. The practical solutions in this book will help you reach your emergency preparedness goals and give you peace of mind.

FOOD

The first five chapters of this book revolve around food. Food is the reason most people embark on a journey of long-term preparedness in the first place. While food is not the most life-threatening survival priority, hunger—and the idea of preventing it—is an immensely powerful motivator, especially to those who rarely experience it. In fact, food (or lack thereof) is the largest weapon of mass motivation the world has ever known.

There is a lot to think about when building your own long-term food storage pantry. By the end of this first part, you will have set your preparedness goals and will understand exactly how much food, and what kind, to purchase to meet those goals. You will understand all of the food options on the market (freeze-dried, canned, bulk goods, and more) and will make decisions about how much of each one to purchase. From planning and purchasing to repackaging and storing, this part will equip you with everything you need to build a practical long-term food storage pantry that is customized to fit your budget, space, goals, and needs.

CHAPTER 1

The Practical Long-Term Food Storage Pantry

FOOD
WATER
HEATING
SANITATION

This chapter will discuss a few foundational elements of long-term food storage that you need to consider before spending too much time or money. As many in the preparedness industry say, failing to plan is planning to fail. This is true with food storage as well. This chapter will go over a few things to consider when choosing and setting up a space to store and organize your food. Each person's available space is different, but the tips in this chapter will help reduce storage headaches down the road as you begin to build out your long-term food storage space and pantry.

This chapter will also outline the tiered system of timelines I use to make sense of long-term food storage. While you might not choose the same timelines for your own storage plan, you will need to decide what your goal is. Without knowing how long you want your food storage to last, it is difficult to put together a solid preparedness plan. I'll help you break down your storage goal timelines so you can make sense of it all.

Making Room for Your Long-Term Food Storage Pantry

Depending on the timeline you are preparing for (I personally keep one year's worth of food on hand), there can be a sizable amount of food involved. You will also be interacting with at least part of your long-term food storage on a regular basis, so it will be designed as an extension of your existing kitchen pantry. Because of these two factors, I recommend choosing a dedicated space to be your long-term food pantry. Mine is a corner closet in our basement.

I realize that it might be difficult to find extra space, but if you get serious about working these concepts into your lifestyle, you will find that a dedicated space will make this process easier to manage. When choosing one, you'll want to consider the following points.

MAKE IT ACCESSIBLE

You want your long-term pantry to be easily accessible. Your long-term pantry will work in conjunction with your kitchen pantry, and you don't want access to your pantry to be a frustrating hassle if you can help it.

TRY TO ELIMINATE THREATS

Threats to long-term food storage include sunlight, heat, moisture, and pests. If you can, choose a location free of all four. I'll teach you how to further protect your food using specific storage strategies later, but

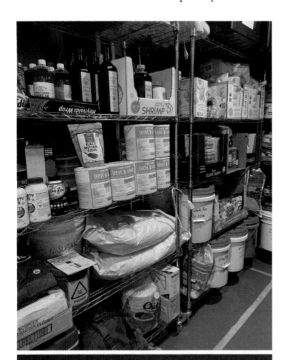

Many types of shelving will work to store your food, but these wire shelves on caster wheels are the ones I prefer.

ONLINE RESOURCE PAGE

There is an extensive online resource page for this book that provides access to additional information, links, videos, training, and more. I reference it numerous times throughout this book. It can be found at www.creekstewart.com/thedisasterreadyhome.

A dedicated space for your food storage is a good idea. My long-term food pantry is located in a corner basement closet under the stairs.

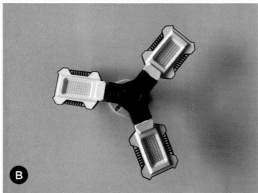

(A) Taking the extra time to ensure good lighting in your pantry is a worthy investment. This is an area where you will be spending time. I installed these recessed can lights, but plug-in flood lights or lamps are good options as well. (B) If your closet already has a light bulb fixture, but does not provide adequate lighting, consider purchasing one of these folding LED light bulbs. They can be expensive, but provide more light in a small space than any other bulb on the market.

where you actually store your goods is the first line of defense.

USE SOLID SHELVING

I have been through many types of shelving over the years. I started with cheap plastic shelves and got what I paid for. I now use six large wheeled wire rack shelving units that cost about $60 apiece. The shelving you use to store your food and supplies can either relieve or add a great deal of frustration to the process of building out a long-term food pantry. At the online resource page for this book (CreekStewart.com/thedisasterreadyhome), you will find links to the shelving units I use and recommend.

INSTALL GOOD LIGHTING

Most closets or basement corners do not have good lighting. I took the time to install additional overhead lighting in my closet pantry, and it has made a world of difference. Fighting the shadows with flashlights is no way to operate in a long-term food pantry. You want the space to be inviting and easy to navigate. It is worth spending the extra money to either install additional lighting or buy some lights that make sense for the space.

HAVE ELECTRICITY AVAILABLE

I have found that having an electrical outlet in the space (or at least nearby) is really convenient. Whether for vacuuming or plugging in tools to help with repackaging bulk goods (see Chapter 3), an outlet nearby is a real bonus.

The Three-Tiered Storage System

Now that we've covered a few tips for preparing your pantry, let's break down the food category of preparedness into a few stages to help you nail down your own goals.

I store roughly one year's worth of food for my family of four. For me to wrap my head around storing that much food, I needed to break it up into chunks. I call these chunks "tiers," and the tiers are based on periods of time (days, weeks, months). In general, my long-term food storage is divided into three tiers. While there is a lot of gray area between these tiers, and quite a bit of overlap, I believe that thinking of your long-term food storage in terms of time periods is extremely helpful. You may want to structure your tiers differently, and that is fine. In the next sections, I'll describe each of my three tiers and the reasoning behind them. Then, I'll ask you to create your own tiers of timelines before moving forward.

CREATIVE STORAGE

Small spaces and apartments can be especially challenging when building long-term food storage. One dedicated room or closet may not be realistic. The alternative is creative storage. Ideal places to tuck away long-term storage items such as bottled water, bulk dry goods, or freeze-dried foods include:

- Under beds
- In chests or drawers
- Back corners of closets
- Behind couches
- On top of kitchen cabinets
- Behind doors
- Unused corners of rooms
- On top of freestanding dressers or wardrobe closets

Almost 80 gallons of water storage are tucked away out of sight in a wooden chest.

TIER 1: FIRST TWO WEEKS

The first tier of my system is simply the food that is in my kitchen pantry, refrigerator, and freezer. Because I do not have a permanent long-term off-grid power supply, I do not consider frozen food to be long-term food storage. I do have a couple of generators, but only keep enough fuel to run these for a few weeks intermittently. We keep roughly two weeks' worth of meals on hand at any given moment in our immediate kitchen pantry. This is a combination of food we eat every day, including:

- Canned goods
- Dry pasta
- Cereal
- Oatmeal
- Fresh and frozen meat
- Milk
- Fresh vegetables and fruits

My grid-tied freezer is full of frozen meat. Because I don't have a long-term off-grid power supply to run this freezer, I do not consider it a part of my long-term food storage.

With this first tier we have a two-week buffer of food before we even need to step foot into our long-term food storage pantry. A two-week food supply is the absolute minimum amount of food every household should have on hand at any given moment.

If you consider a freezer to be a part of your long-term food storage, then you must be prepared to power that freezer long-term as well. This was an expensive problem for me. The least complicated solution was to not consider frozen food as part of my long-term storage. We always have a lot of frozen food, especially wild game, but I do not include this food in my long-term food storage calculations. If we don't lose power, it will be bonus food in my stores.

This is what three months' worth of freeze-dried food looks like for my family of four.

TIER 2: TWO WEEKS–THREE MONTHS

I figure if a disaster strikes and forces a shelter-in-place scenario for more than two weeks (without any access to outside food), then something awfully bad is happening. It is likely that one would need to focus on many different priorities at the same time, such as power, first aid, communications, heating, hygiene, security, and more. In that case, I want to have the option for simple turnkey meals to make life easier during a difficult transitional phase that is far from normal. Because of this, I have planned for three months' worth of prepackaged, freeze-dried meals to provide a simple, stopgap meal solution for me and my family. I'll discuss freeze-dried meals later, but they are essentially "add hot water" camping meals that require very little effort, thought, or time to prepare.

For this two-week to three-month period, I have three freeze-dried meal servings per day for all four members of my family. This equates to roughly 900 freeze-dried meal servings. Depending on the company used and the food purchased, the cost of this can easily exceed $1,500. This is a lot of money to spend on freeze-dried food, but keep in mind that I accumulated these meals over several years, spending $100 at a time. Freeze-dried meals will also last twenty-five-plus years, so it is an investment that will not go to waste anytime soon. They can also be used while hiking, camping, or even during a disaster bug out.

I am fully aware that some family budgets do not allow for expensive freeze-dried meals, and that is fine. You do not need to own a single freeze-dried product to have long-term food storage. In fact, everything mentioned in my three-month to one-year tier can fill this tier as well. The freeze-dried meals simply provide ease of use, solid nutrition, and variety during a period that will very likely be stressful and chaotic.

TIER 3: THREE MONTHS–ONE YEAR

Although anything I have planned for Tier 3 can easily be consumed during a Tier 1 or Tier 2 timeframe, I have reserved Tier 3 foods for

---

BUG OUT VERSUS BUG IN

"Bug out," or "bugging out," is the decision to leave your home in the event of a large-scale disaster. Oftentimes, the best decision is to leave, or "bug out," to a safer location. Alternatively, the decision to stay at home during a disaster scenario is to "bug in," or "shelter in place."

the latter portion of my one-year food storage plan. Tier 3 is made up of essentially two categories of food:

The first category of food in Tier 3 is the deep storage of shelf-stable foods you already eat on a regular basis. Most shelf-stable grocery goods have a shelf life of anywhere from one to three years. These products include:

- Canned vegetables
- Soup powders
- Nut butters
- Oatmeal
- Cereal
- Pasta
- Boxed meals
- Packaged meals
- Canned soups
- Soup mixes
- Oils
- Snacks
- Candy
- Canned meats
- Canned tuna

This category does not include anything fresh, such as produce, meats, eggs, or baked goods that spoil quickly. All my goods in this category have an expiration date of at least one year out, preferably longer.

The second category of food in Tier 3 is bulk dry goods that are repackaged at home specifically for long-term food storage. These are goods that are carefully

ENEMIES OF LONG-TERM FOOD STORAGE

There are certain factors that notoriously degrade, ruin, or shorten the storage time for long-term food and water products. Regardless of how or where you keep your items, always try to reduce or eliminate the following threats:

- **Oxygen:** Oxidation can be prevented primarily through the use of oxygen absorbers. We will discuss these in detail later.

- **Moisture:** Keep your stored food away from moisture at all costs. We'll discuss packaging solutions that will help with this.

- **Pests:** Pests such as bugs, weevils, and rodents can infest your food and water if you're not careful.

- **Heat:** The optimal storage temperature for most stored foods is under 72°F.

- **Sunlight:** Sunlight increases storage temperatures, and the ultraviolet rays degrade packaging. With water, sunlight can also encourage algae growth.

repackaged to last twenty years or longer. While they can easily be worked into a weekly rotation cycle in the kitchen, I treat most of my bulk dry goods as true survival food and do not plan on cracking them open until a worst-case scenario. We will dig into the details of this category and the repackaging process in Chapter 3, but it includes foods such as instant oats, rice, peas, lentils, whole-wheat berries, flour, quinoa, pasta, dried beans, and many other types of grains and seeds that can be made into or incorporated into meals. Many of these items can be purchased in 25- or 50-pound quantities for significant money savings over your regular grocery store items and freeze-dried foods.

(A) I will teach you how to properly repackage 25- and 50-pound bulk bags of dry goods into 5-gallon buckets for long-term food storage. (B) All items on the middle shelves are part of my regular food rotation plan. These are foods that we buy at our local grocery store and eat on a regular basis. This "deep stock" of rotation food items makes up a very large portion of our long-term food storage.

PLANNING YOUR OWN TIERS

Timed tiers are not necessary to amass long-term food stores—they just make sense for me. At this point, take a minute and decide if you will be dividing your food storage into hypothetical timed tiers. Use this chart to detail each tier.

1	
2	
3	
4	
5	
6	

The Importance of Rotation

Before we discuss calculating how much food to buy, I want to briefly introduce a key element in the long-term storage plan. The biggest mistake most people make when it comes to long-term food storage is buying a bunch of food and eventually having to throw it away because it expires. My goal is to make sure you never do this, so we will be using a food storage strategy known as *rotation*.

Ideally, the majority of your long-term food storage will consist of items and ingredients that you and your family eat on a regular basis. You should identify the foods you eat most often and then stock up on these items (likely over many weeks or months) so that you have a built-in buffer of food in your long-term food storage pantry. As you build your own larder of food, you will begin to "shop" from your own long-term pantry when you run out of items in the kitchen. You will use the oldest items first and replenish your long-term pantry on your routine grocery runs. This rotation strategy only works if you store the food you eat and eat the food you store. Chapter 2 will discuss rotation in more detail, but it is important you at least understand the basic concept early on. Rotation is a key part of a workable long-term food storage plan.

Going to the grocery store and stocking up on random food items for long-term food storage is not a workable strategy. The next chapter will outline a series of calculations and rules for purchasing food. These rules will help you make sense of buying large quantities of food and give structure and intention to your food purchases.

FOOD

WATER

HEATING

SANITATION

CHAPTER 2

How Much Food Will You Need?

This chapter covers the ground rules that can simplify the sometimes-overwhelming process of long-term food storage. In full transparency, these rules are based on assumptions, estimates, and generalities. If you follow them to build one year's worth of long-term food storage, you may be off by a month or two. This is an acceptable variance for me. If you want to be as exact as possible with your amounts and timelines, the methods in this chapter will give you a solid base to start from.

Your Storage Goal

Although you can certainly start building a long-term food storage pantry with no goal in mind, I believe it helps to pick an overall timeline. If you are just starting out and do not know where to begin, I'd recommend a minimum of three months' worth of long-term food storage. If you are feeling pretty serious about this subject, then choose six months or one year. If you completed the tier timeline table in Chapter 1, then you likely already have an overall timeline in mind.

Choosing a timeline to work toward not only helps you set short-term goals and budgets; it also gives you security in knowing how long you can feed yourself and your family if disaster strikes. In the following space, set your long-term food storage goals by writing in the overall timeline you are currently preparing for.

OVERALL TIMELINE

Calculation Ground Rules

Once you have established a timeline, it's time to figure out how much food you need to fill it. To make this process as easy as possible, here are some ground rules.

GROUND RULE #1:
Treat Everyone As an Adult

Except for infants still on milk or formula, I treat everyone as a full-sized adult. I initially tried calculating kids' servings versus adults' servings and found it very difficult, so I simplified it and made everyone an adult. This solved a lot of problems for me. The bonus is that you will likely end up with more food than you need. That is a good problem to have in most cases. In the space that follows, write how many adults you are preparing to feed.

NUMBER OF ADULTS

FOOD TYPE	NUMBER OF SERVINGS PER MEAL	DAILY NUMBER OF SERVINGS
Grain	x3 =	
Protein	x3 =	
Vegetables/Fruit	x3 =	

GROUND RULE #2:
Each Meal Consists of One Serving of Grain, One Serving of Protein, and One Serving of Vegetables or Fruit

Is this a perfectly balanced diet? Maybe not, but it is close enough and it's certainly better than nothing. Using this ground rule means that I need four servings of grain, four servings of protein, and four servings of vegetables or fruit three times a day (twelve servings of each, total) for my family of four.

In the table on this page, write how many servings of grain, protein, and vegetables/fruit you need per meal (that is, how many people you are planning to feed). Then, multiply these numbers by three to get your total number of servings of grain, protein, and vegetables/fruit per day.

GROUND RULE #3:
Use Food Labels to Count Servings

For any food product that has the number of servings listed on the packaging, use that number in your serving calculations. If the product lists a half size, such as 3.5 servings, round that number down. I realize that some manufacturer serving sizes are small and some are large, but for the sake of simplicity, I just take the label at face value and add it to my goal total.

GROUND RULE #4:
1 Cup = One Serving

Almost all bulk dry goods, such as oatmeal, rice, beans, and grains, are sold by weight instead of serving size—for example, in 25- or 50-pound bags. In the case of bulk dry goods, I consider 1 cup of reconstituted food to be one serving size.

I take food label servings at face value. For example, this can of green beans shows 3.5 servings. For simplicity, I round down all half-serving sizes, which in this case means three servings of vegetables.

WHAT IS A NO. 10 CAN?

If you are just getting started in food storage, it is important you understand what a No. 10 can is. "No. 10," "#10," and "Ten-Pound Can" are all terms used synonymously to describe the same size can. The phrase has nothing to do with how much of something it will hold. It is simply industry lingo for the can size. A No. 10 can is $6^3/16$ inches in diameter by 7 inches tall and will hold different amounts, depending on the food items. It will hold roughly 109 ounces of liquid but far less of whole freeze-dried strawberries. Different-sized cans are denoted with different numbers; for example, the 20-ounce can of pineapple chunks in the photo is referred to as a No. 2 can. No. 10 cans have become very popular packaging cans within the long-term food storage industry. They are a great size for storage and are very durable.

Here are two common size cans: a No. 2 can of pineapple chunks (left) and a No. 10 can of freeze-dried blueberries (right).

GROUND RULE #5:
⅓ Cup Bulk Dry Goods = 1 Cup Cooked

Although some bulk foods vary slightly, ⅓ cup of dry goods is a fairly good estimate for what you'll need to make 1 cup of reconstituted cooked food that is ready to eat. For example, ⅓ cup dry rice equals about 1 cup cooked rice. Using this estimate you can quickly calculate how many cups of food product you need to meet your serving goals for the timeline. It might not be exactly perfect for some bulk dry goods, but it is close enough for most.

GROUND RULE #6:
Use Food Weights to Determine How Much Bulk Dry Goods You Need

On the online resource page for this book, you will find my Bulk Food Weights Download Sheet. This is a downloadable Excel spreadsheet for you to use to help in this process. On this sheet I have provided you with the ⅓-cup weights for almost every available dry bulk good that you'll ever consider incorporating into your long-term food storage. You can use these weights, combined with how many ⅓-cup servings you will need, to determine the total weight of dry bulk goods you will want to keep on hand for your goal time period.

Simple Calculation Example

Following is a simple real-life example of how I used this system to determine my long-term food storage breakfast needs for one person for one year.

1 Serving of Grain

- ⅓ cup instant oats = 1 cup cooked oatmeal
- ⅓ cup instant oats weighs 0.07 pounds (taken from Bulk Food Weights Download Sheet)
- 0.07 pounds of instant oats × 365 breakfasts in 1 year = roughly 25 pounds of dry bulk instant oats

1 Serving of Protein

- 1 (28-ounce) jar of my favorite peanut butter contains 25 servings
- 365 breakfasts in a year divided by 25 servings = roughly 15 jars of peanut butter

1 Serving of Fruits/ Vegetables

- 1 No. 10 can of freeze-dried apples contains 20 servings (12 ounces)
- 365 breakfasts in a year divided by 20 servings = roughly 19 No. 10 cans of freeze-dried apples

Here is one year's breakfast supply for one person using the given calculation examples: 25 pounds of bulk instant oats, 15 (28-ounce) jars of peanut butter, and a combination of No. 10 cans of freeze-dried fruit and bags of dried fruit.

Three Broad Categories of Long-Term Pantry Food

So far we've discussed the importance of choosing a preparation timeline and some ground rules for calculating how much food you will want to store. Now let's discuss the food itself. Chapter 3 will go into more detail on these food categories, but for now you should understand that there are essentially three categories of food you'll be storing:

1. Freeze-dried foods
2. Bulk dry foods (typically sold by the pound)
3. Food from the grocery store, just like the stuff you eat every day (these products typically have serving quantities on the product labels)

Bulk dry goods (beans, rice, whole-wheat berries, lentils, and so on) will last just as long as freeze-dried foods if repackaged properly at home and stored in ideal conditions. These are true survival-style food products and can be treated as such and essentially forgotten about until needed. While you can allocate large portions of your long-term food storage to these two categories, the most practical and useful long-term food storage pantries are very heavy on the "grocery store" category.

Why? Because this is the food that you eat every day. This is the food that already makes up your normal diet. It's the food that you are most familiar with eating and preparing. And it is the easiest to buy and shop for. Most people go to the grocery store at least once a week, maybe more. This brings me to my final long-term food storage ground rule.

Ground Rule #7: Don't Break the Rotation Rule

When it comes to buying grocery store food products, do not buy and store food you do not eat on a regular basis. If you do, you run the risk of having to throw it away and completely waste your time and hard-earned money. As mentioned earlier, most shelf-stable packaged foods in the grocery store have a shelf life of one to three years, so if you buy them, put them on a shelf, and do not eat them, you will have to throw them away.

It may be tempting to load up on canned goods and other products because they are inexpensive or on sale, or seem like good survival foods. You tell yourself you'll eat them before they expire, but I can tell you from experience that you will not. Chances are you will only eat the foods you are used to and like from your long-term pantry. As tempting as it might be to buy thirty jars of lime marmalade because you can get them for 25 cents a jar, don't do it. (Unless, of course, you eat lime marmalade several times a week!)

A long-term food storage pantry that is deep on just a few products you really like is much more practical (and cost-effective) than a long-term food storage pantry that has a bunch of different foods that you never eat. This is because you are much more likely to *rotate* through the foods you love, so you'll never have to throw anything away because it is expired.

My suggestion is to list the top ten to twenty shelf-stable food products that you and your family eat on a regular basis (foods with expiration dates of one to three years off). Ten of my family's top twenty are:

- Peanut butter
- Canned green beans
- Canned olives
- Jars of spaghetti sauce
- Jars of pickles
- Canned chicken
- Canned tuna
- Boxes of macaroni and cheese
- Boxes of almond crackers
- Bags of dried dates

This list becomes a big portion of your long-term food storage. You will build your long-term food storage pantry by slowly building your

HOW TO SAVE MONEY

Long-term food storage is a financial investment. Not breaking the rotation rule will save you far more money than buying foods at a huge savings that you will never eat.

YOUR TOP TEN

In the spaces that follow, write your top ten shelf-stable grocery store foods (expires in one to three years) that you and your family eat on a regular basis. Bulking up on these ten products is a good place to start when building your long-term food storage pantry.

1	
2	
3	
4	
5	
6	
7	
8	
9	
10	

own in-house stock of these items. As you build this stock (as time and budget allow), you will begin to rotate through these products before they expire. You will essentially go shopping from your own long-term food storage pantry and replenish those items on a first-in, first-out basis from the grocery store. This process of rotating through the foods you already eat and building up a sizable stock of those items at home is the lifeblood of a very practical and effective long-term food storage plan.

CHAPTER 3

Long-Term Food Preservation Methods

FOOD

WATER

HEATING

SANITATION

This chapter will dig deeper into the main types of food you'll use to build out your long-term pantry. You'll learn the pros and the cons of each type so you can gauge what is best for you and your circumstances. By the end of this chapter, you'll be equipped to start making some serious decisions about how your long-term food pantry will be structured.

Freeze-Dried Food Products

Freeze-drying is an amazing food preservation method. It is the process of removing water by first freezing the food. Then air pressure is reduced, and heat is added back in. This combination causes the frozen water to turn straight to vapor. The technical word for this is *sublimation*. The moisture vapor is then removed from the chamber, leaving the food completely dried.

Freeze-dried foods have a shelf life of twenty-five-plus years. And almost any food imaginable can be freeze-dried, including eggs, cooked meals, milk, fruits, vegetables, candy, meats, fish, herbs, spices, cottage cheese, guacamole, pie, salsa, ice cream, and the list goes on and on. There are only a few foods that do not freeze-dry well. Most of them are heavy in oil such as butter and peanut butter.

Most camping meals are freeze-dried these days. The company Mountain House dominates the market with these meals, and they can be found in almost every camping and outdoor store. They

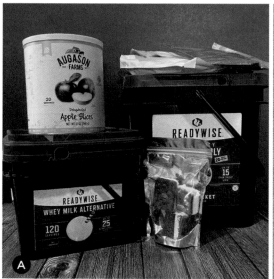
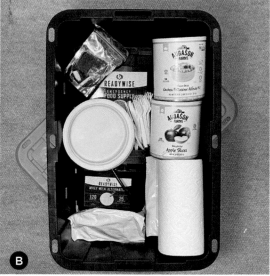

(A) I stock a variety of freeze-dried meals in various types of packaging in my long-term food storage pantry. Large buckets are a very common packaging option for bulk freeze-dried meals. (B) My two-week food tote contains enough freeze-dried meals to feed me and my family of four for two weeks if we ever needed to leave the house in a hurry.

are great for camping because they are extremely lightweight and can be reconstituted with just boiling water, typically inside of the packaging in which they are sold. Most single-serving meals require you to pour a cup or so of boiling water into the package and wait 10 minutes for it to be ready to eat. It doesn't get much easier than that.

Freeze-dried meals make great options for bug out bags because of the weight and convenience of preparation. I've included freeze-dried meals in my own bug out bag for years. I also have a tote in my long-term food storage pantry called the "two-week food tote." This grab-and-go tote contains two weeks' worth of freeze-dried meals for me and my family if we would need to suddenly evacuate our home. This is extra food above and beyond what is packed inside of my bug out bag. A two-week tote of food provides a lot of peace of mind and weighs only about 20 pounds.

Several large companies sell freeze-dried food products specifically for long-term food storage. I've listed the ones I recommend at the online resource page for this book. There are even at-home freeze-dry machines available. I've included links to those as well at the resource page. Almost all the companies that sell freeze-dried products sell variety packs of entrée meals and buckets or cans of single-food items such as apples, meats, milk, and vegetables. The entrées available include Cheesy Pasta, Chicken Noodle Soup, Potato Pot Pie, Beef Stroganoff, Teriyaki and Rice, and more.

WHAT IS A BUG OUT BAG?

A bug out bag is a backpack of gear, food, water, and other supplies to get you through three days of independent survival in the event that you have to evacuate your home during a large-scale disaster. It has everything you need to survive for 72 hours without access to stores, electricity, water, or restaurants. It is designed to help you get from point A to point B during a disaster.

My three-day bug out bag gets me from point A to point B.

You can even buy meal kits based on timelines, such as a 1-Month Survival Meal Bucket that includes three freeze-dried meals each day for thirty days.

One could argue that freeze-dried foods are the perfect long-term food storage product:

- The process maintains almost all the food nutrients.
- The food stores for twenty-five-plus years in the right conditions.
- Freeze-dried foods can easily reconstitute with just water.

If your goal is to "set and forget" your long-term food storage, then freeze-dried foods should definitely be a big part of your mix. Because of the extremely long shelf life, freeze-dried food does not require rotation and can be a hands-off approach to long-term food storage.

There are two big drawbacks to stocking up on freeze-dried foods for your long-term food storage pantry. First is the price. Unfortunately, the cost of all that convenience and storage life is not cheap. This is by far the most expensive type of long-term storage food. I had to accumulate my freeze-dried food buckets over many years as my budget allowed. I have even been known to ask for freeze-dried food buckets for Christmas. (I am a survival nerd like that.) The second drawback is not a huge deal but something to at least be aware of. If you store only freeze-dried meals, it can be a shock to your system to suddenly switch from your normal diet to one entirely made up of freeze-dried survival meals. Although freeze-dried meals are totally healthy, even for long-term consumption, many report that constipation is a common side effect. So, consider adding some fiber to your long-term food plan if you go deep on the freeze-dried options. Fiber supplements such as Benefiber or Metamucil are easy options to consider.

I have had this 52-serving freeze-dried meal bucket from ReadyWise in storage for many years.

Pros and Cons of Freeze-Dried Food

Following are some pros and cons you should think about when considering freeze-dried foods:

Pros

- The process maintains more than 90 percent of food nutrients.
- There are no added chemicals or salt.
- The shelf life is twenty-five-plus years.
- Food maintains its flavor.
- Almost any food can be freeze-dried, so there is a huge variety of freeze-dried food in the marketplace.
- Products are very lightweight and typically packaged in easy-to-store buckets.
- Meals are easy to prepare by adding hot water (typically into the packages the food comes in).

Cons

- It's the most expensive type of long-term food storage on the market (you pay for all those pros).
- Some people experience constipation when suddenly shifting to a diet of freeze-dried food.

Canned Goods

Canned goods purchased from the grocery store are the easiest and most accessible long-term food storage products in the marketplace. This category also includes other shelf-stable products available at the average grocery store, such as boxed dinners, beef jerky, and dry cereal. Most of the items in this category have a shelf life of one to three years before they expire. Expiration dates and number of servings are conveniently listed right on the packaging to take out any guesswork.

For most people, this category of food will make up a large portion of a long-term food storage pantry. However, because these foods expire in three years or less, they must be entered into a regular cycle of rotation. Consequently, long-term food pantries that are deep in

Some of my shelf-stable grocery store food items for rotation include canned beans, canned meats, dried fruits, spaghetti sauce, apple cider vinegar, coconut oil, and peanut butter.

these types of foods are *not* "set it and forget it" pantries. These are what I call "lifestyle pantries" because they work day-in and day-out with your new long-term food storage lifestyle. If you do not want to incorporate a system of rotation into your lifestyle, then do not buy deep on products that will expire in three years or less.

The real key to this category of food is to store only those food products you eat most often. The list you created in Chapter 2 of the top ten shelf-stable food products your family eats on a regular basis can be the beginning of your long-term food storage pantry. Your goal is to stock up on these products each time you go to the grocery store. Buy a few extra here and a few extra there until you have a decent stock of your most popular products at home. A calculation of grain, protein, and fruit/vegetable serving numbers will give you an idea of how long the food you have on hand will get you through, if necessary. You will continue building stock until you have enough on hand to get you through your goal timeline.

As you accumulate these shelf-stable items, you'll continually put the new purchases in your pantry and take out the oldest items for day-to-day use. It's that simple. Any food products from the freeze-dried category or bulk dry goods category would obviously be calculated into your serving counts as well.

ORGANIZING FOOD

There are several important notes I want to share about this category of food based on my experiences using it to build my own long-term storage pantry. Stacking a few cans or boxes of food in your kitchen pantry is easy and requires no thought. But stacking eighty cans of green beans on wire shelving is another story altogether. I've tried all kinds of ways to organize my rotation foods. The method I've landed on

is to stack and organize each type of product in its own open-faced cardboard box on my wire shelving units. While you can probably make your own, you can also get them at wholesale clubs and some grocery stores for free. Stacking cans, bags, boxes, and jars is much easier inside cardboard walls than just out on the shelf, and the box prevents them from toppling all over the place—and, in the case of glass jars, shattering.

(A) I keep extra open-faced cardboard storage boxes in my long-term food storage pantry. (B) I use open-faced cardboard boxes to store, stack, and organize my canned goods and other grocery store items on my shelving racks. These are a simple and very low-cost way to get started.

I write larger, more visible "best by" dates on food packaging with a Sharpie marker for easy visible inventory management.

FIRST-IN, FIRST-OUT

When organizing packages of food in your long-term food storage pantry, be sure to do so in a way that encourages a first-in, first-out rotation cycle. When you "shop" from your long-term pantry, you want to always pull the oldest product first so that you keep everything safely within your expiration deadlines.

PROMINENT EXPIRATION DATES

I mark my "best by" dates prominently on the packages when I store them so I don't have to hunt for them later. I typically do this with a Sharpie marker on the front part of the box or on the top of the can. This helps me keep my products in the right order.

EXPIRED CANS

While I cannot officially recommend that you eat canned goods that have expired, I can tell you that I have done so many times. I can also tell you that many industry experts I have talked to say that canned food lasts far longer than the "best by" dates on the cans. From what I can tell, the consensus is that if the can isn't dented, bulging, leaking, or corroding, then the food is likely still good. Your own judgment of sight and smell will, of course, tell you a lot as well.

DENTED CANS

Do not buy dented canned goods. This was taught to me by my friend Jesse Alphin, who has a degree from Virginia Tech in agriculture and life sciences–food safety. The reason is that a swollen can is one of the first signs that the food inside has gone bad. If you purchase a dented can and the food causes the can to swell, it may only pop out the dent and still look totally normal. Inspect all your cans for long-term food storage. Cans with a sharp crease/point in the dent could mean that the airtightness has been compromised and should be avoided as well. For the same reasons, cans accidentally dropped and dented/creased at home should be used as soon as possible.

BUY A GOOD CAN OPENER

A friend (thank you, Robin Passey) gave me this tip. Buy a backup industrial-grade manual can opener to keep with your long-term food storage. Even if you use a manual can opener now, grab an extra super-duty one just in case. I've included the link to the one she recommended to me at the online resource page for this book.

This industrial-grade Swing-A-Way can opener is available online.

Bulk Dry Goods

Bulk dry goods are foods, typically seeds or grains, that can be purchased in bulk in large bags or buckets. This is likely the category that will be least familiar to most people. While you may have purchased 1-pound bags of rice or beans at the grocery, not many people have purchased 50-pound bags of rice, lentils, oats, elbow pasta, or whole-wheat berries. However, bulk dry goods can potentially make up a massive portion of your long-term food storage pantry. Items such as beans and rice can be huge supplements to your grain and protein servings. While these dry foods can be incorporated into a regular rotation schedule, these goods are typically purchased and stored for long-term survival only. In fact, a free PDF publication by the Federal Emergency Management Agency (FEMA) titled *Food and Water in an Emergency* (www.fema.gov/pdf/library/f&web.pdf) states that whole-wheat berries, dried corn, soybeans, pasta, and white rice all have an indefinite shelf life when properly stored. I would argue there are many more dry bulk foods that do as well.

If packaged and stored properly, bulk dry foods can last as long as freeze-dried foods. One of the big advantages is that bulk dry goods are

Here's a new shipment of bulk dry foods in my food storage pantry. These include yellow corn, popcorn, quinoa, whole-wheat berries, quick oats, white rice, and millet. The bags they come in are not suitable for long-term storage. Each item must be carefully repackaged to protect the investment for many years to come.

very inexpensive in comparison. In fact, just a few hundred dollars' worth of bulk beans, lentils, and rice can feed a family for several months. These items, along with some spices for flavoring (discussed later) are always my suggestions for people who are looking for some quick long-term food storage and are on a very tight budget. Bulk dry goods are a perfect option if you want to pack away some last-ditch survival food on a budget.

LEARN MORE ABOUT BULK DRY FOODS

In the Grains and Protein sections in Chapter 4, I will detail an entire laundry list of bulk dry foods that you can buy (and where to get them).

Bulk dry foods are especially susceptible to moisture, oxygen, pests, and sunlight. These seeds, beans, and grains are durable when stored properly but extremely vulnerable when not. The problem is that most of these goods are sold in large paper bags or, if you are lucky, a cheap plastic bucket. This may work for restaurants or large catering companies that will use the goods within a few days, but it does not work for the long-term food pantry enthusiast who wishes to stash away said goods for twenty years or more. The good news is that I will teach you how to store these items in a way that keeps all the threats at bay. The process outlined in the next section will give you peace of mind in knowing that the investment you have made (in time and money) in your long-term food storage is protected for many years to come.

How to Repackage Bulk Dry Goods for Long-Term Storage

The best container for repackaging bulk dry goods is a 5-gallon plastic bucket with a waterproof lid—they are cheap, readily available, and stack well. They also help protect the food inside from three of our four main threats—water, sunlight, and pests. However, they do not protect your food from oxygen. Because of that you will need an oxygen barrier and absorber. This is why we use Mylar bags and oxygen absorbers.

Mylar was developed by DuPont in the 1950s and revolutionized the food packaging industry. It is technically a metalized polyester—a polyester bag coated in aluminum. This combination makes the bag a superior barrier against moisture and gases, including our nemesis oxygen. When you package bulk dry goods in Mylar bags and then pack them inside durable sealed plastic buckets, you can essentially create a time capsule of food and a microclimate of protection around it. Following is the step-by-step process I recommend for repackaging.

PURCHASING MATERIALS

Purchase the plastic 5-gallon buckets from your local hardware store. A food-grade bucket is best but not necessary because of the Mylar lining you will be using. I purchase my buckets from stores like Lowe's, Home Depot, or Menards. I also include some links to online bucket sources at the online resource page for this book. You will also need to purchase lids. I suggest spending the extra few dollars on what is called a gamma seal lid. This type of lid is unique in that the center screws out and gives you easy access to the contents without having to remove the lid. This is a convenience, not a necessity. If you are on a tight budget, you can opt for a regular lid. While you're shopping, you'll also need a rubber mallet to seal the lids (either style) and a bucket wrench for getting the lids off once they're on. If your local hardware store does not have a bucket wrench, just do a quick online search for "bucket wrench," and many options will pop up. I have also included these links at the online resource page.

(A) A 5-gallon food-grade plastic bucket with a gamma seal lid can be used as a storage container for bulk dry foods. (B) Once the outer ring of the gamma seal lid is snapped onto a bucket, the inner portion of the lid can be screwed out for convenient access to the food inside.

You will also need to purchase Mylar bags and some oxygen absorbers to seal inside with your food. The Mylar bags keep oxygen out once you seal your food inside. The oxygen absorbers soak up any oxygen that you seal inside of the bag with your food. You will need to buy either 5-gallon or 6-gallon Mylar bags (6-gallon bags give you a little more wiggle room but are not necessary). Oxygen absorbers come in many different sizes for different-sized containers. The size you will need for 5-gallon buckets is 2000cc. Often you will find Mylar bags and 2000cc oxygen absorbers sold together. You can find these online at MylarPro.com and PackFreshUSA.com. I also have quick links for you at my online resource page.

Once you have these supplies and your dry bulk goods, you are ready to repackage.

(A) Tools needed to repackage food in 5-gallon plastic buckets include a rubber mallet for hammering on the lid and a bucket wrench for getting the lid off. (B) A 5-gallon Mylar bag acts as an oxygen barrier to protect the food stored inside plastic containers. (C) This vacuum-sealed package contains 2000cc oxygen absorbers that will be opened and placed individually inside Mylar bags with food. These will absorb any trapped oxygen inside the Mylar bag with the food. These must be kept sealed until ready for use.

OPENING AND RESEALING A MYLAR BAG

Dry bulk foods will easily last for several months after a Mylar bag has been opened. There is no immediate need to reseal a Mylar bag once you start using the food inside. However, if you forgot to put in an oxygen absorber and need to cut open a sealed bag, or if you want to open and reseal a Mylar bag for any other reason, it can be done. The best way to do this is to cut off an upper corner of the bag as shown in the photo. Then, when you are ready to seal it back up, the air can easily be sucked out, a new oxygen absorber placed inside, and the corner sealed with a home iron as described in this chapter.

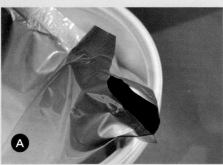

(A) Cut corner of Mylar bag.
(B) Resealed corner of Mylar bag.

Prepping Your Bucket

Put your bucket on a sturdy work surface, put your Mylar bag inside, and spread it open in the bucket a little bit. You do not have to be too meticulous about this because the weight of the food will do most of the work.

Filling Your Bucket

Pour your dry bulk food (grains, beans, rice, pasta, and so on) into the Mylar bag, shaking the bucket a little bit as you go to help the food settle. Fill the bucket to within about 2 inches from the top. Toss one 2000cc oxygen absorber right on top.

Sealing Your Mylar Bag

1. Place a 2 × 4-inch or 2 × 2-inch board across the rim of the bucket. This creates a smooth, solid surface against which to seal your bag.
2. Neatly fold the top of the Mylar bag across and over the board and smooth it out with your hands.
3. Mylar seals with heat, and the best tool I have used for the job is a home clothes iron set on the cotton setting. Start in the middle and work your way out to each side. You'll see the Mylar seal as you run the hot iron over it. Leave about a 3-inch opening in the Mylar bag before you completely close out the second side.
4. Use a Shop-Vac or vacuum cleaner hose to suck out as much air as you can

STEP 1

STEP 2

STEP 3-A

STEP 3-B

STEP 3-C

STEP 3-D

STEP 4

STEP 5

from the bag, then quickly seal up the last 3 inches with the hot iron. As long as you keep the tip of your Shop-Vac or vacuum cleaner hose several inches away from the dry goods you will not run the risk of sucking any up.

STEP 4
Closing Your Bucket
Neatly tuck the top of the Mylar bag into the bucket and use the rubber mallet to hammer the rim of the gamma seal lid into place. You have to hit it surprisingly hard to make sure the lid is pushed down to the seal. You will know when it is seated correctly because it will snap into place. Then, screw in the center of your gamma seal lid.

STEP 5
Labeling Your Bucket
Finally, label your bucket with the following for easy visual inventory in your long-term food storage pantry:

- Date of packaging
- Quantity of contents

You can write right on the bucket with a Sharpie marker or use a label or duct tape. Once done, these buckets are ready to store in a cool, dry place out of direct sunlight. Once opened, there is no need to replace the oxygen absorbers or reseal the Mylar bag as long as you plan on eating the food within several months. As long as they are kept away from moisture, sun, heat, and pests, dry bulk foods are shelf stable for months on their own.

KILLING INSECTS, INSECT EGGS, AND LARVAE

Like it or not, there are live insects, insect eggs, and/or larvae in pretty much all bulk dry food goods. It's just a fact of life. They can be microscopic and undetectable to the human eye at the time of storage. Over time, they can hatch, grow, reproduce in and feed on the food inside of a bulk packaged container. I take two measures with my bulk packed food to help prevent this from happening and destroying my investment of time, materials, and money.

1. Oxygen absorbers are the first step in preventing insect infestation. Sucking out available air as described and then reducing the oxygen within the sealed Mylar bag with oxygen absorbers creates an environment that is not easily compatible with life, even for insects.
2. I place each of my bulk packaged containers into a chest freezer for three days. In fact, I have a small chest freezer in my basement dedicated for this purpose that I purchased for $50. It fits three 5-gallon buckets perfectly.

Neither step is 100 percent effective at killing all insects, eggs, or larvae, but when combined, they have worked very well for me over the years.

Diatomaceous earth (DE) is also an option to kill insects in food storage. Diatomaceous earth is a powder made from ground fossilized remains of a plankton called diatoms. This powder has been used for a very long time to deter, control, and

A glass Mason jar with an airtight canning lid is the perfect storage solution for fresh oxygen absorbers.

kill insects. The sharp edges of these ground remains cut through the insect's exoskeleton and cause it to dry out and die. It does not work on insect eggs and only works on insects with an exoskeleton. According to a Utah-based supplier of DE (www.diatomaceousearth.com), 2 teaspoons of DE should be used for every pound of stored food. The powder should be mixed directly with the dry food at the time of storage. Learn more at www.diatomaceousearth.com/blogs/learning-center/diatomaceous-earth-protect-food-storage.

Dry Canning in Jars

I'll be the first to admit that I'm not a home canner. My mom is and my grandma was, but it is just not in the cards for me. However, I do can quite a bit of dry bulk foods using a process called *dry canning*. Dry canning uses the same Mason jars with the metal lids and screw-on bands as regular canning (or you can reuse glass jars from the grocery store that used to contain things like olives, jam, or spaghetti sauce). Plastic containers are not recommended because they will not provide a barrier to oxygen over time. With dry canning, you are applying the same principles used with storing in Mylar bags and buckets.

Start by placing your dry goods in a clean, dry glass jar. For your average quart-sized canning jar, add a 300cc oxygen absorber and then screw on the lid for a tight seal. If your jar lid has a safety pop-top lid,

I store dry-canned bulk foods in glass Mason jars and other recycled food jars. This method of storage is perfect for smaller quantities, and foods will store just as long if kept in a cool, dry area away from sunlight.

OXYGEN ABSORBER CHART	
CONTAINER SIZE	**ABSORBER SIZE**
½-Pint	50cc
Pint	100cc
Quart	300cc
Gallon	500cc
5-Gallon	2000cc–2500cc

then the oxygen absorber will likely draw the lid down over the course of 30 minutes and you will not be able to pop it. This is a good sign that you have a tight seal. Be sure to store these jars in a cool, dry area that does not get direct sunlight.

The chart can help you determine what size oxygen absorbers you need for different volume containers.

FOODBRICK STORAGE CONTAINERS

A unique and feature-rich food storage container to consider for your long-term pantry is the FoodBrick. Unlike the less expensive improvised storage containers such as 5-gallon buckets, the FoodBrick is a true storage system with infinite storage flexibility. FoodBricks not only stack efficiently as a cube, but they can be stored individually as well and work great in closets or under beds. A stack of ten 3.5-gallon FoodBricks is the equivalent of a 35-gallon drum and can hold up to 270 pounds (2,640 adult servings) of dry bulk goods. For long-term food storage (years versus months), it is still important to use Mylar bags and oxygen absorbers in the same way you would with 5-gallon buckets. Check out the FoodBrick storage system at WaterBrick.org.

I use FoodBrick containers to store dry bulk goods such as rice, pasta, and beans.

Extending the Use of Bulk Dry Goods with a Grain Mill

While we're on the subject of bulk dry goods, one tool to consider adding to your long-term food pantry is a manual hand-crank grain mill. For the small investment, this one tool can give you many more options with your bulk dry goods in the kitchen. A hand-crank grain mill allows you to grind almost any bean, lentil, seed, or grain into a meal or flour. You can turn dry rice into rice flour, beans or lentils into flour for quick soups or spreads, corn into cornmeal for cornbread, whole-wheat berries into flour tortillas, and more. The options are endless and become especially interesting if you are looking for gluten-free baking ingredients. You can even use the mill to grind wild foraged acorns into a very nutritious acorn flour, like I do.

My son uses a Roots & Branches grain mill to grind rice, lentils, and beans into a unique multipurpose flour.

The manual grain mill I use is from Roots & Branches (you can find a link at the online resource page for this book, but many different brands will do the trick). This one is on the lower end of the price scale. More expensive, more durable hand-crank brands include Lehman's Own, Wonder Mill Junior, and Country Living. Hand-milling is a really fun experience, and it is surprising how much flour you can produce in just a few minutes of grinding.

CHAPTER 4

Types of Food to Store

FOOD

WATER

HEATING

SANITATION

Now that you've learned how to calculate your food quantities and considered your options when it comes to storage, preservation, and packaging, you can now spend some time detailing the food itself. There are many different types of food that could go into a long-term pantry, but most of what you will need falls into six main categories: grains, protein, fruits and vegetables, fats, flavorings and spices, and vitamins. This chapter will detail each of these categories, and by the end you will be equipped with a great list of food product ideas to choose from to fill your pantry.

Grains

Over half of my long-term food storage is made up of items in the grain category. Grains provide an array of important nutrients in our diet. These include carbohydrates, many valuable vitamins, and several minerals such as iron, magnesium, and selenium. In addition, grains are an important source of dietary fiber, which helps prevent constipation. Grains are perfect for filling out a meal and are typically quite easy to prepare. Oatmeal, for example, can be a meal in and of itself. Add some peanut butter for protein and a serving of raisins or dried apples, and you have a delicious and nutritious survival breakfast in just a few minutes using only hot water.

An advantage of grains is that they can be stored long-term (twenty-plus years) using the 5-gallon bucket storage process outlined in Chapter 3. They do not have to be entered into a rotation cycle. Think about which ones make sense for you and your family. Download the Bulk Food Weights Download Sheet at the online resource page for this book to determine how much of each you need to fill your daily servings for your goal time period and begin to chip away at stocking up, one Mylar-lined bucket at a time.

Most of my bulk dry grains are stored in 5-gallon buckets or FoodBricks on lower shelves in my long-term pantry.

Grains to consider for long-term food storage include:

- Amaranth
- Barley, hulled or pearled
- Buckwheat
- Couscous
- Dry corn
- Durum wheat berries (whole)
- Flax
- Hard red and hard white wheat berries (whole)
- Kamut
- Millet
- Oats (oat groats, rolled oats, quick oats)
- Popcorn
- Quinoa
- Rye berries
- Soft white wheat berries (whole)
- Spelt
- Triticale
- White rice (Brown rice has a shelf life of only a few years due to its high oil content. Do not store brown rice unless it's entered into a rotation cycle.)

FREE RECIPES FOR BULK DRY GRAINS

While I will not be listing specific recipes using various grains in this book, I do have a free book download, *Bug Out Bag Recipe Book*, available at the online resource page for this book that details over fifty quick and easy recipes using dry bulk goods and grains during a disaster scenario.

Download the free *Bug Out Bag Recipe Book* for over fifty recipes using dry bulk grains.

My family's pasta storage includes over 100 pounds of spaghetti in rotation on our grain shelving unit and a deep stock of mac and cheese. This section is my kids' favorite.

APPETITE FATIGUE

"Appetite fatigue" is the name for the feeling you get when you're tired of eating the same thing repeatedly. Appetite fatigue can cause even hungry people to not want to eat. Keep this in mind when storing food in your long-term pantry. Intentionally include variety to prevent potential appetite fatigue.

PASTA

I consider pasta to be a part of the grain category and store it in the same way. Pasta is the most popular food in the world and at the top of the list for comfort foods. All different sizes, shapes, and varieties of pasta are perfect for long-term food storage. A growing supply of gluten-free pastas are even available in bulk. Different pastas can be used to make an infinite number of meals to reduce appetite fatigue. From macaroni and cheese and pasta salad to mushroom-stuffed shells and ramen soup, you are limited in pasta dishes only by the number of flavorings and sauces you can whip together. I have deep storage of elbow pasta, bow tie pasta, spaghetti, orzo, ramen noodles, and others.

BULK DRY GRAIN SOURCES

There are several places you can go to buy your bulk dry grains. Here is a rundown of my favorite places, but keep in mind this list is not inclusive, and you may find other sources that work better for you.

Warehouse Stores

The convenience of shopping at warehouse stores like Costco, Sam's Club, and BJ's is hard to deny. Most online companies have steep shipping fees that must be factored into the budget, and bulk dry goods aren't lightweight like freeze-dried foods. Warehouse stores stock a huge array of dry goods that can be purchased in quantity and repackaged at home. I purchase most of my pasta, instant oats, and white rice from stores like these.

Restaurant Supply Stores

Gordon Food Service (GFS) is a regional restaurant supply chain in my area that also sells to the public. Check here if there is one in your area: GFS.com/en-us. If not, there are bound to be similar restaurant supply stores that sell in bulk to the public not far from you—you may just have to do some research to find one. I have purchased many bulk goods from GFS, including pasta, beans, lentils, and spaghetti. They also carry large cans of shelf-stable sauces, fruits, vegetables, and just about anything else you'll find on the menu at a restaurant.

Country Life Natural Foods

Country Life Natural Foods (www.countrylifefoods.com) is a wholesale and retail distributor of natural, organic, and vegetarian foods. They are based in Michigan and have a service that delivers for free if you are in their shipping zone. There is a truck that runs through my area in Indiana every couple of weeks. They have a mind-boggling supply of bulk dry goods. I have ordered instant oats, rice, popcorn, yellow corn, and even millet from them. If you are in their delivery area, you can save quite a bit of money on shipping.

LDS (Church of Jesus Christ of Latter-Day Saints) Storehouse

The Mormon Church has one of the largest networks for purchasing bulk foods and long-term food storage products that exists, and as of this writing you do not have to be a member of the church in order to buy the products. You can visit their online shop or find out if there is a store-house location near you here: https://providentliving.churchofjesuschrist .org/food-storage. They offer bulk bags of dry goods such as whole-wheat berries and also a huge variety of freeze-dried food. Their prices are about as good as it gets for this type of food.

Rainy Day Foods

Rainy Day Foods (RainyDayFoods.com) offers a great selection of bulk foods. Their sixteen-bean mix and ABC soup mix are both good choices.

Azure Standard

Azure Standard (AzureStandard.com) delivers bulk goods all over the country. They can ship through carriers like UPS, but they also deliver to over three thousand drop points all over the country. You can have your order delivered to one of these "drops," where you can pick it up. They have a huge selection of bulk grains and specialize in organic and non-GMO products.

Online Retailers

While not the best-priced suppliers, online retailers like Amazon do carry many of the items listed in this category, and shopping with them can be very convenient.

Protein

According to the United States Department of Agriculture, all foods made from seafood, meat, poultry, eggs, beans, peas, lentils, nuts, seeds, and soy products are part of the protein foods group. Some of these foods are feasible for long-term storage and some are not. This section will detail the food items I stock to fill the protein servings in my pantry and give you plenty of options to pick from for stocking your own.

Freeze-dried meats are expensive, so I also store plenty of beans, chickpeas, and lentils. I do stock several buckets of freeze-dried meats, but most of my protein servings are made up of dry beans, dry

(A) I keep a couple shelves of protein rotation products, including peanut butter and canned beans. (B) Freeze-dried meat buckets from ReadyWise can remain indefinitely in my long-term food storage pantry.

chickpeas, dry lentils, canned meats (in rotation), canned tuna (in rotation), peanut butter (in rotation), and a dried soy-based protein called textured vegetable protein (TVP). Following is a non-exhaustive list of protein items to consider for your pantry:

- **Freeze-dried meats and seafood:** Meats and seafood are the most expensive freeze-dried food, but they are also a very dense food when it comes to nutrition. I stock several buckets of freeze-dried meats, which I have invested in over time. I offer a variety of my favorite brand of freeze-dried products on my website at CreekStewart.com/food.
- **Dehydrated meats (beef jerky):** Most dehydrated meats have a one-year or less

shelf life, so they must be entered into rotation. Beef jerky is my weakness, so we have this in the kitchen and long-term rotation pantry.

- **Freeze-dried powdered milk**
- **Freeze-dried eggs**
- **Nuts:** Nuts, such as walnuts, peanuts, almonds, pecans, and hazelnuts, are excellent sources of protein. However, because of the oil content, they go rancid too quickly for long-term storage, so they should only be considered as a part of regular rotation. We stock walnuts, almonds, and peanuts in rotation; they are primarily eaten as snacks and oatmeal additions.
- **Peanut butter (and other nut butters):** This is definitely a rotation product because of the oil content, but spoonfuls of peanut butter can be added to oatmeal and many other dishes, not to mention peanut butter and raisin sandwiches made with fresh-baked hand-milled bread. I use peanut butter in my oatmeal every morning, and the kids love PB&J sandwiches, so rotating through peanut butter is no problem for our family. For peanut-sensitive families, almost any kind of nut butter is available these days, including sunflower seed butter. They are more expensive, but at least you have options.
- **Dry bulk beans:** There are many varieties of beans to consider for long-term food storage. Some of the most popular include black turtle beans, garbanzo beans (chickpeas), black-eyed peas, kidney beans, fava beans, pinto beans, navy beans, lima beans, and mung beans. Not only can beans be cooked and eaten, but they can also be ground into meal and made quickly into a refried bean–like texture. They can also be ground into a fine powder and added to soups, stews, tortillas, or breads. I buy most of my bulk dry beans, split peas, and lentils from a local restaurant supply store and repackage them all in 5-gallon buckets with Mylar bags.
- **Dry bulk peas and split peas:** While not nearly as high in protein as most beans, peas can add variety to many dishes and are great additions to salads and pastas.
- **Dry bulk lentils:** Lentils are in a food group all their own and go well with rice and in soups and curry dishes. Lentils typically come in brown, red, and green and have a somewhat peppery flavor.

One great way to create a meal from beans, peas, and lentils is by making a multi-bean and lentil soup. This soup includes water, dried beans, and a blend of seasonings. Bob's Red Mill has a great soup mix seasoning recipe at www.bobsredmill.com/recipes/how-to-make/bean-soup-seasoning.

- **Canned beans, peas, and lentils:** All of these items can be purchased, cooked, and canned at the grocery store and are good sources of protein. However, when purchased precooked like this, these products must be entered into rotation because of the one- to three-year shelf life. We keep at least 100 cans of various beans on hand at any given moment and use them for making chili, tacos, rice bowls, bean salads, red beans and rice, and more. Beans can also be a side dish in and of themselves.

(A) I repackage black-eyed peas in Mylar for long-term storage. (B) I store lentils in 5-gallon buckets, FoodBricks, and glass jars. All will last twenty-plus years.

At the time of this writing, a 50-pound bag of textured vegetable protein stock (TVP) can be purchased for under $60, then stored in 5-gallon buckets or FoodBricks.

- **Textured vegetable protein (TVP):** TVP is made from soybean flour and is an excellent source of protein. It is also an excellent candidate for 5-gallon bucket/Mylar bag long-term storage, where it will last for many years. TVP is an extremely popular meat substitute among vegetarians and can be used in tacos, chilis, stews, and more. It flavors easily and reconstitutes from its dehydrated state in hot water in 10 minutes. I stock about 100 pounds of TVP in 5-gallon buckets. I do not eat TVP on a regular basis and consider it survival food only. There are great ideas to consider on the Bob's Red Mill website at BobsRedMill.com/tvp-textured-veg-protein.html.

- **Protein powder supplements:** Many people these days add some form of protein powder to pancakes, biscuits, and morning smoothies. If you use protein powder, this can be a great item to add into rotation to boost protein intake during a shelter-in-place scenario. It will not store long-term, but if you rotate it regularly you can build a stock of some backup powder for a rainy day. There is an incredible assortment of protein powders on the market that can accommodate almost any diet or sensitivity. These include powders made from soy, whey, and peas. Many grocery stores now have large sections dedicated to protein powders.

Fresh Meat and Fresh Eggs

Although fresh meat and eggs are not long-term food storage items, this category is a big part of some people's long-term food plan. A small flock of three to five backyard chickens can keep a family in fresh eggs for many months with minimal effort and maintenance. I have friends who raise meat rabbits with great success. I have other friends who have put their efforts into raising tilapia fish on their back porch using an aquaponics system. Small-scale "backyard" farming can produce a renewable source of food across several categories, so it is something to consider if you have the space and interest. We currently have a small flock of four chickens that we raised from chicks. The kids absolutely love them, and they live in a coop that we move around in our backyard.

Raising backyard chickens can be an incredibly fun hobby as well as a long-term food project. Kids especially love caring for chickens. We've raised these hens from chicks, and they will be laying eggs in a few months.

RAISING CHICKENS

Backyard Chickens (BackYardChickens .com) is a great place to start if you are interested in raising chickens. I also have an article on getting started with chickens here: ArtOfManliness .com/skills/manly-know-how/ how-to-raise-backyard-chickens.

Most chickens start laying eggs at about eighteen weeks and will lay reliably for two to three years. After that, egg production will start to become less frequent. Once this happens the chickens can be used as a source of meat.

We move our chicken coop around in the backyard every few days to provide our chickens with fresh forage.

Fruits and Vegetables

Fruits and vegetables provide amazing resources for the human body, including vitamin A, potassium, folate, vitamin C, dietary fiber, and so much more. For many long-term food pantries, fruits and vegetables, especially fresh ones, are a real weak area. If you are a gardener and home canner like my mother and grandmothers, then your pantry is likely filled with beautiful glass jars of green beans, jams, asparagus, beets, and more. But home canning is not as popular as it once was. Access to fresh and factory-canned produce, along with affordable prices of these products, has reduced the need for home canning over the years. I home can a little bit, but not nearly enough to put away stock for long-term storage.

The flip side of home canning is that you must have the produce to can. This means you must grow the fruits and vegetables yourself or buy them locally or from the grocery store. Even for those who garden, four-season environments eliminate access to fresh produce for half the year if grocery stores or delivery is not available. The good news is there are still options for the preparedness-minded person, even if you don't do canning and even if you don't have a big garden.

A can of freeze-dried apples is an excellent long-term food store product, and also a great snack.

Here is a mix of ideas to consider for the fruit and vegetable servings of your long-term food storage:

- **Freeze-dried fruits and vegetables:** Freeze-dried fruits, especially, are delicious. Apples, strawberries, and bananas make excellent additions to oatmeal and breads. I stock these mainly in cans because they are so easy to store and are a manageable size once opened. I've been known to grab a No. 10 can of freeze-dried apples for snacking on a long road trip. I also have at least forty cans of shredded or sliced freeze-dried potatoes. They are perfect as a simple potato side or made into potato soup, hash browns, potato cake, and more. I have even run the shredded potatoes through my manual grinder to make potato flour. I don't have the space to grow potatoes in my raised beds, and my family eats a lot of them, so this is one freeze-dried product I've invested in. I also have several 5-gallon buckets of freeze-dried vegetables. These include peas, green beans, corn, and a few others—I only buy the vegetables that I know my kids will eat. Mixing freeze-dried peas

I store packaged fruits and vegetables on a wire rack in my long-term food pantry. This section mainly houses rotation fruits and vegetables such as green beans, corn, beets, olives, spaghetti sauce, and raisins.

with macaroni and cheese is a sneaky way to fit in a vegetable serving for the kiddos.

- **Dried fruits:** We eat quite a bit of dried fruits, such as apples, mangoes, apricots, raisins, figs, and dates. We buy all of these in large bags from warehouse stores. These won't store long-term, but we do stock several bags of each and have them in our rotation cycle. They are great for snacking. Again, if you do not eat something like dried fruit on a regular basis, don't store a bunch of it long-term because it will likely go to waste later.

- **Canned fruits and vegetables:** By far, most of my fruit and vegetable long-term storage is canned goods from the grocery store. While we prefer eating fresh produce as a family, I intentionally work canned produce into our diets to enter these products into a forced rotation because it is important for me to have them in our long-term food storage pantry. With that said, we only stock the items we eat regularly. The kids dictate this list primarily. We keep thirty to one hundred cans of each of the following on hand: French-cut green beans, olives, corn, asparagus, pickles, and pickled beets.

- **Spaghetti sauce:** I count spaghetti sauce as a vegetable. We sampled many different grocery-bought spaghetti sauces until we found one everyone liked, then we went deep on it. We stock in rotation glass jars of spaghetti sauce that our warehouse store stocks in two-packs. We

LONG-TERM FOOD STORAGE FOR PETS

Humans aren't the only ones in the household to consider when building your long-term storage pantry. Dog, cats, and other pets should be taken into consideration as well. Most dry dog and cat foods are not dry enough for long-term storage in Mylar bags with oxygen absorbers. The moisture content makes even the dry food very susceptible to mold. In addition, the high oil content can cause the dry food to go rancid over time. Although a Google search for "freeze-dried pet food" will reveal countless options that will last fifteen-plus years, this is a very expensive route. The most practical long-term food solution for your pets is to build stock of their normal food as budget allows and enter it into rotation just as I have described previously for your own regularly consumed foods.

We buy two-packs of spaghetti sauce at our warehouse store and repurpose the empty jars for dry-canning lentils.

eat a lot of spaghetti with sauce, so rotation is not an issue (we also rotate the spaghetti). I repurpose all the glass jars for dry canning other products such as beans, spices, and other dry bulk goods that I can stuff in a pantry crack and forget about for a while.

- **Sprouting seeds:** A robust sprouting plan is one strategy I'm most proud of when it comes to prepping for vegetables. Stocking a healthy supply of seeds for sprouting into fresh greens on your kitchen table fills a huge gap in the long-term food storage category of fresh produce. In fact, I have dedicated the entire next chapter to teaching you about survival sprouting during a shelter-in-place scenario, including my six-day sprouting cycle and exactly what seeds to have on hand. For now, just know that you can easily sprout a large amount of delicious and nutritious fresh greens on your kitchen counter with no experience, no sunlight, no soil, and no green thumb.

Fresh Produce

Besides sprouting, storing fresh produce is not practical for the long-term food storage pantry. That said, some fresh produce, such as apples, squash, pumpkins, potatoes, beets, carrots, and turnips, will store very well for many months in a cool, dry area like a cellar. This is where the term *root cellar* comes from. In fact, as I am writing this book in May, my mom has hundreds of root vegetables, squash, and apples stored from last fall in a corner room of her basement. Root cellars were the original "cans," and this is exactly how generations of people all throughout the world got through the winter with fruits and vegetables—and many still do.

Even though not everyone has the space or land for a large garden, I would argue that anyone can grow at least something to contribute to their food independence or long-term food storage. An extremely small raised bed garden—say, 4 feet square—can produce an astonishing number of vegetables in just one growing season. Mel Bartholomew's book *Square Foot Gardening* is a particularly good read on the square-foot-gardening concept and will make you think about gardens in a whole new way. For example, up to eight of the following plants can be planted in just 1 square foot of space:

- Green beans
- Turnips
- Beets
- Cilantro
- Peas
- Garlic
- Leeks
- Onions
- Tomatoes
- Spinach

(A) My parents store a variety of vegetables on the cool, dry basement floor. Shown here are pumpkins, squash, sweet potatoes, potatoes, and onions. These will last many months. (B) This is the salad section in one of my raised garden beds in late April. These greens can be harvested multiple times a week for the next five to six months.

Even patio pots on a sunny balcony can produce a surprising harvest of vegetables. Herbs are perfect candidates for even smaller pots on a windowsill. While growing your own food is not technically considered long-term food storage, having your own system of food production means there will be fresh food even when food storage runs out. Raised bed gardens and patio pots require little time, space, or money to implement and should be at least considered as a part of your long-term food storage plan.

Wild Foraged Food

Foraging is a bit off-topic with regard to long-term food storage, but it is still worth mentioning for consideration as a facet of your overall survival food plan. Before modern canning, freeze-dried food, and raised bed gardens, our primitive ancestors foraged all their food from the landscape. Wild plants and wild game can be remarkable food resources for the knowledgeable and experienced forager. Foraging is certainly not as easy as going to the grocery store, but wild food will exist long after the grocery store shelves go empty.

LEARN MORE ABOUT FORAGING WILD FOOD

While I can't teach you all you need to know about foraging wild food in this book, I would like to recommend two resources if this is a subject you'd like to dig deeper into. First, I have a service called Wild Edible Plant of the Month Club (WildEdiblePlantOfTheMonth.com) where I teach about a new wild edible plant every month. This is a great way to learn how to identify, harvest, prepare, and eat wild edible plants. Second is an online course, taught by an expert trapper friend of mine, specifically about survival trapping using a modern steel Conibear trap: OutdoorCore.com/courses/how-to-set-conibear-trap.

Fats

Fat gets a bad rap. Fats are essential to the human body and support a myriad of important health functions. Nature itself tells us a lot about the importance of fat. Every predatory animal I can think of eats the fattiest parts of its kill first, and sometimes exclusively. Often, what we would consider the best and choice cuts of meat are left behind entirely.

Fats absolutely need to be included in the long-term storage pantry. The big problem with storing fat is that heat, light, and oxygen break down fat and cause it to go rancid. Rancid fat is not only nasty to eat but is also harmful to the body. An odd odor and unusual discoloration are the top two signs that fat has gone rancid.

Fats do not store well long-term, but they are very easy to work into a regular cycle of rotation so that you can still have plenty on hand for many months of uncertainty. The typical storage life of most fatty products is one to two years. Here is a breakdown of what fats I keep on hand to give you some ideas for your own pantry.

- **Coconut oil:** Compared to most fats, coconut oil has a very long shelf life—some even say it's indefinite. Even so, this is a fat product that is in a regular rotation for me and my family. We keep enough for one year on hand and use it primarily as a cooking oil. Coconut oil can easily be worked into your long-term diet as a butter substitute, melted into coffee or tea, or added to baked goods. I buy mine at the grocery store or warehouse store and keep several large jars on hand.
- **Olive oil:** Olive oil is a staple for my family. We use it in almost every fresh salad we make, including fruit salad, pasta salad, and bean salad. We drizzle it on chicken, fish, tuna, and other meats. We use it on roasted vegetables and often substitute it for butter in other dishes. It has a shelf life of about one year, so it is definitely a rotation product, but moving through it has never been an issue for us.
- **Canned tuna, salmon, and sardines:** Cold-water oily fish are an excellent source of omega-3 fatty acids and also high in protein—a double-win for sheltering in place. They are easy to eat on their

A few of my stored fats include coconut oil and olive oil.

RANCID FAT: A FUNNY STORY

When we were dating, my wife-to-be made a big deal of cooking a special dinner for me. She bragged about how good she was at making spaghetti. Long story short: She used rancid olive oil in the marinara sauce, and it tasted like gasoline. I can report firsthand that you definitely do not want to eat rancid olive oil. And, serving it is not a great way to win over someone you might fancy.

own or incorporate into meals, as they mix well into just about any dish or can be a stand-alone serving of protein. The shelf life of canned fish is normally between one and three years, which is great for rotation. The pull-top lids combined with not having to cook the contents make these little cans one of the easiest survival meals to eat. You'll never find me on a campout or hike without a few cans of tuna or sardines. That, some dried dates, and crackers is my go-to lunch in the wild. In fact I probably eat more canned sardines in one week than most people have had in their lifetime.

- **Nuts and nut butters:** Even though I've listed nuts and nut butters in the protein category already, these double as excellent sources of fats. All of them have to be entered into rotation, but a couple spoonfuls of nut butter is a very easy way to intake fats. Wild foraged and store-bought nuts such as walnuts, acorns, hazelnuts, pecans, and hickory nuts are also excellent sources of healthy fats.

- **Butter:** Butter is an excellent source of fat and can be added to just about anything. The only problem with traditional butter is that it does not store long unless kept in the refrigerator or freezer. Two work-arounds to this I have found are dehydrated butter powder and canned butter. Augason Farms sells a 2-pound, 4-ounce can of dehydrated butter powder that has a shelf life of ten years. These are very affordable, and I keep several in my long-term food pantry. Dehydrated butter can be reconstituted with water and used like traditional butter, or it can simply be added as is to baking recipes, pancakes, mashed potatoes, and macaroni and cheese. It is also perfect sprinkled on popcorn and fresh-cooked vegetables or meat. Red Feather sells canned butter (not dehydrated), which has a shelf life of ten years. Both products are available online.

Flavorings and Spices

Flavorings and spices are not necessarily a food category, but their importance in long-term food storage is often underestimated. It is this category that turns the many hundreds of pounds of dry bulk goods such as beans, grains, and rice into actual meals. Without them, appetite fatigue is just days away. A small assortment of dried herbs and spices can add an almost infinite variety of flavor to bulk dry goods.

Dry spices do not go bad over time; they just lose their potency. This makes them an odd storage item. I do not rotate most of the spices and flavorings I store because, quite frankly, we don't cook with spices all that much, and many of the spices I've purchased are designated to add variety to the dry bulk foods like beans, rice, and grains in storage. The spices and flavorings I do have in rotation include honey, maple syrup, dried garlic flakes, dried onion flakes, garlic salt, garlic powder, everything bagel seasoning, and our favorite barbecue sauce (Rufus Teague). Pretty much all my other spices I have on a five-year update plan. You will notice I said five-year "update plan" and not "replacement plan." This is because I do not throw away the old spices. I simply put them all into a 5-gallon bucket, label them as "Old Spices" with the date, and store them away just in case.

Before I list some spices and flavorings to consider, I'd like to share a few tips and tricks I've picked up over the years when it comes to this category:

- Spices tend to store best in the original airtight packaging they are sold in. I have never found a reason to repackage spices that are already sold in glass or plastic bottles.
- When possible, store spices in their whole form (for example, whole peppercorns versus ground pepper). Whole spices store significantly longer than their ground counterparts.
- The enemies of spices are the same as for other foods: oxygen, sunlight, heat, and moisture. Do your best to store them in the absence of all of these.

This section of my long-term food storage pantry contains spices and other flavorings.

- Bulk spices purchased in paper or plastic bags should be repackaged in Mylar bags with the appropriately sized oxygen absorber or using the dry canning process described in Chapter 3.
- Dollar stores and discount variety stores often have name-brand spices for cheap.

Here is an assortment of spices and flavors that I stock, along with my personal insights, for you to consider:

- **Honey:** Honey is a forever food. We eat quite a bit of honey as a family, and I keep honey in rotation even though it will last forever. Honey may crystallize over time, but that does not mean it is bad. Getting a beehive is on my list of things to do this year, and I am very excited to be able to harvest our own honey as a part of our long-term food plan.
- **Maple syrup:** I also have maple syrup in rotation. It is a sweetener we use every morning in oatmeal and is a great alternative to white sugar. We also tap several maple trees each spring to boil down small batches of our own syrup.
- **White sugar:** Sugar is another forever food—it stores very well long-term. However, oxygen absorbers tend to turn it into a brick. Use desiccant packets instead, or nothing at all. I buy sugar by the bulk bag at my local warehouse store. I store around 150 pounds of sugar in Mylar bags inside 5-gallon buckets.
- **Dried garlic flakes, dried onion flakes, garlic powder, garlic salt, everything bagel seasoning:** I stock all of these spices in bulk and use them in rotation. These are the most common spices we use for cooking.
- **Barbecue sauce:** We do not use a lot of barbecue sauce, but my kids love it on chicken, so I stock it in rotation. It would be great to season anything from rice to wild game.
- **Fresh chives, oregano, cilantro, basil, mint, lavender, rose hips:** We grow all of these culinary herbs in either patio pots or raised beds in our backyard. Even the annuals reseed themselves and come back each year. They are wonderful fresh while in season but are easily dried and stored for use in the fall and winter until the fresh versions come back up. Rose hips soaked in apple cider

vinegar (an item we also stock in rotation) and mixed with olive oil makes our favorite salad dressing, which we use almost exclusively. Mint makes an amazing tea. Cilantro is great for any kind of tacos, and oregano and basil add flavor to pasta and spaghetti sauce.

- **Salt:** I consider salt to be one of my most important stored flavorings. I store over 200 pounds of it in various forms, including sea salt, regular table salt, and pink Himalayan salt. Salt will last almost indefinitely without any additives. It is the one thing I do not store inside Mylar bags or metal containers because of its corrosive nature. Instead, I store salt either directly in plastic 5-gallon buckets with a gamma seal lid or in plastic zip-top bags and then inside plastic 5-gallon buckets. Salt has a forever shelf life on its own and does not require oxygen absorbers for long-term storage. I also have plenty of salt just sitting around my long-term food storage pantry in its original grocery store packaging. I buy all my salt at the local grocery or warehouse store.

- **Peppercorns:** I purchased enough whole peppercorns to fill one 5-gallon bucket and packaged them in a Mylar bag with an oxygen absorber. Pepper is an important spice, and I feel confident these peppercorns will store for thirty-plus years. I still purchase normal containers of ground pepper as needed for everyday use. I can use my bulk stored pepper at any time if I want, but I consider it a long-term storage product and plan to use it only if normal pepper from the grocery is unavailable. Alternatively, you could store a year's worth of normal pepper containers or peppercorns and use them in rotation.

- **Chicken bouillon:** Bouillon cubes or granules can add flavoring to just about any meal or food. It is a fantastic and versatile survival flavoring to keep on hand. According to the FEMA publication *Food and Water in an Emergency* (FEMA.gov/pdf/library/f&web .pdf), all bouillon products have an indefinite shelf life. However, I would only give most bouillon products a few years because of the oil content. If you use bouillon on a regular basis, then entering it into rotation could make sense for you. We do not use bouillon that often, so I have opted for cans of dehydrated chicken bouillon from RainyDayFoods.com. The cost is under $40 and includes over 1,400 servings per can, with a twenty-five-year shelf life. This was the best solution for our circumstances. Almost every one of my survival kits and bug out bags has a handful of chicken bouillon cubes. Hot water and a chicken bouillon cube make a great broth base for just about any meal in the wild, especially wild greens.

- **Various herbs and spices:** A few other flavorings that I stock in small amounts are dried thyme, dried rosemary, chili powder, red pepper flakes, ground cumin, and ground cinnamon.
- **Spice mixes:** Spice mixes for specific flavor profiles are a great addition as well. These include taco seasoning, Italian seasoning, chili seasoning, Cajun seasoning, chili powder, curry powder, and everything bagel seasoning. Large plastic containers of these ready-mix spices can be purchased at warehouse stores.
- **Drink mixes, coffee, and tea:** Coffee, for many people, is a daily staple. Fresh-ground coffee and coffee beans are not suitable for long-term food storage. However, an interesting fact that many people do not know is that most instant coffees are in fact freeze-dried coffee. If the consistency is crystal-like, then it is freeze-dried

(A) Here are some of the spice mixes I stock up on. **(B)** Drink flavorings I keep on hand include coffee, a variety of teas, and Tang.

and will last for many years if left in the original airtight container. I purchased several cans of instant freeze-dried coffee from my warehouse store as a long-term coffee solution. Powdered drink mixes for kids are also a great item to consider for long-term storage. I have found powdered drink mixes like Tang to be good long after the "best by" date.

Vitamins

Let's face it, long-term food storage diets do not typically win awards for nutrition. With all the other calculations we must make when planning, it is a miracle to not forget a large food group altogether. However, if you ever find yourself in a shelter-in-place scenario, it is important to take the extra step to make sure your body is getting everything it needs to stay strong and healthy and fight off sickness. A daily regimen of vitamins is an important part of this.

When it comes to vitamins, I keep it simple. I make sure to have a year's supply on hand of the daily vitamins that my family and I take. Our vitamins have a one-year shelf life, so it is quite easy to keep this product in a regular rotation cycle. Vitamins are like spices; they lose potency over time but don't necessarily become unsafe to consume.

Other immune-boosting supplements and vitamins to consider stocking for this category include:

- Vitamin A
- Vitamin C and/or Emergen-C
- Vitamin E
- Zinc
- Iron
- Selenium
- Elderberry
- Echinacea
- Airborne

FOOD

WATER

HEATING

SANITATION

CHAPTER 5

Survival Sprouting

What if I told you that you can grow nearly all the fresh greens you would ever need in a shelter-in-place scenario with no garden, no pots, no dirt, no experience, no outside space, no garden tools, no planters, no fertilizer, no electricity, and even no sunshine. Would you believe me?

It's true. This chapter will teach you survival sprouting. It is the process of taking stored beans, lentils, and seeds and sprouting them on your kitchen table into fresh greens (sprouts) that are packed with vitamins, nutrients, and minerals. What is even more incredible is that you can build a never-ending renewable supply of these greens in only six days, working less than 5 minutes per day. You can do this for one person or an entire family with virtually the same amount of effort.

What Is Sprouting?

Sprouting is the process of soaking seeds for several hours, then rinsing them with clean water a couple times a day until they start to grow and sprout a tail. You have likely seen sprouts sold at the grocery store or even had them served on salads or sandwiches.

Sprouting seeds, legumes, nuts, and grains has a rich history with ancient cultures and first peoples. Sprouting not only makes these foods more digestible, but in many cases increases the bioavailability of nutrients. Seeds themselves are designed to be a mini fortress, protecting what is inside. Often, when you eat seeds, they pass right through your digestive tract and offer you nothing in return. But when you turn these seeds into sprouts, it is another story altogether. When sprouted, a seed is no longer a seed. It is a fresh green. Sprouts are known to have higher concentrations of vitamins and minerals than even the full-grown versions of the same plants. They are

These fresh sprouts grew on our kitchen counter in just six days and are now ready to harvest.

a superfood for the cooped-up survivor and are what some call the "missing link" in long-term food storage.

Supplies Needed for Survival Sprouting

Sprouting is virtually impossible to screw up. Essentially, you need only four things to start sprouting. First, you need a jar. I use wide-mouth 1-quart glass Ball or Mason jars, but any type of jar will work, even plastic ones. It is important to use jars with wide mouths because it's easier to get the sprouts out when finished.

Second, you need mesh jar lids that allow water to drain after the rinsing process (described later). Plastic or stainless steel lids that fit wide-mouth jars are available online. I have links to the ones I use at the online resource page for this book. While these lids are very reasonably priced, you can also make your own by rubber-banding some fine-mesh fabric over the mouth of the jars.

Finally, you will need seeds to sprout and a supply of clean water.

(A) I use wide-mouth 1-quart glass canning jars for sprouting. (B) A variety of mesh sprouting lids, both plastic and stainless steel, allow drainage and airflow to the seeds. (C) You can make your own mesh sprouting lid using rubber bands and fine-mesh fabric purchased from your local fabric store.

Sprouting Seeds

There is a long list of seeds, nuts, legumes, and grains that can be sprouted into greens. It is likely you are already stocking many of these as dry bulk goods in your long-term pantry. How cool is it that you can multifunction the same grains and beans you are currently storing into sprouts? In addition to staples like whole-wheat berries, beans, and lentils, I advise keeping a good stock of seeds on hand specifically for sprouting. I stock six 5-pound cans of dedicated sprouting seeds, which I buy from True Leaf Market (TrueLeafMarket.com/collections/wholesale-sprouting-seed). I store mung beans, alfalfa seeds, red clover seeds, lentil mixes, salad mixes (alfalfa seeds, radish seeds, mung beans, green lentils), and protein mixes (garbanzo beans, adzuki beans, mung beans, green peas). I have listed the links to my favorite seed mixes at the online resource page for this book.

The cans I buy are sealed with oxygen absorbers. There is no reason why these seeds should not germinate ten-plus years from now if unopened and stored in a cool, dry place. Thirty pounds of sprouting seeds will keep me and my family supplied with nutritious fresh greens for many months if we ever needed to shelter in place that long. Even when opened, these No. 10 cans of seeds will last for many months if kept in a cool, dry place.

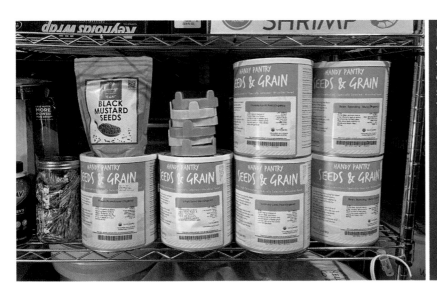

I stock sealed cans of dedicated sprouting seeds in our long-term food storage pantry. These should easily last ten-plus years.

Here is a list of popular sprouting seeds that you may want to consider stocking in addition to your existing stock of bulk dry grains, beans, and seeds:

- Alfalfa
- Amaranth
- Buckwheat
- Clover
- Lentils
- Millet
- Mung Beans
- Oats
- Radish
- Rye
- Soybeans
- Sunflower
- Wheat Berries (whole)

The Six-Day Survival Sprouting Cycle

I sprout my seeds on a six-day cycle, which means I harvest my sprouts on the sixth day of sprouting. With only six jars and six sprouting lids, you can have a never-ending supply of sprouts if you start a new jar of sprouts every day and harvest each jar on the sixth day of sprouting. Each jar is cleaned and cycled back into the six-day rotation with a fresh batch of seeds after each harvest. Twelve jars can give you two jars of sprouts per day, eighteen jars can give you three jars of sprouts per day, and so on. Each 1-quart jar yields several cups of ready-to-eat (or cook) sprouts.

The miracle of sprouting is how little effort the entire process takes, and the almost immediate payback. Following, I have detailed my six-day sprouting cycle so you can replicate it yourself at home.

THE NIGHT BEFORE DAY 1

The evening before your first day of sprouting, put your Day 1 seeds on the soaking deck. Put the seeds in one of your jars, cover them with clean drinking water (tap water is fine) by a couple of inches, and let them soak overnight. When using small seeds, like alfalfa or clover, put in 2 tablespoons of seeds. When using large seeds like garbanzo beans or mung beans, use ½ cup.

(A) Day 1 seeds in between rinses. Notice the saucer used to catch residual water. (B) If you are using a lid without legs, position the jar at an angle.

DAY 1

Morning: Put a mesh sprouting lid on your Day 1 jar of seeds and drain out the water. This water is perfect for using to water patio pots or raised garden beds. Cover the seeds by 2–3 inches of fresh water, swirl them around in the jar aggressively to rinse them, and drain out the water again. Spin the jar to disperse the seeds a bit. Turn the jar upside-down so it will continue to drain and place it in a shaded spot out of the sun. A dark corner of your kitchen counter or inside the kitchen pantry is perfect. Room temperature is ideal. Consider placing the jar in a bowl to catch residual drainage. The plastic screw-on lids I recommend have legs to keep the mouth of the jar propped up for airflow. If you are using rubber-banded lids or lids without legs, lay the jar at a diagonal in the bowl to allow both drainage and air flow.

Evening: Cover the seeds by 2–3 inches of fresh water, swirl them around in the jar aggressively to rinse them, and drain out the water. Place the jar upside-down (or at an upside-down diagonal) back in the cool, shaded area.

Note: If you want to sprout more than one jar of seeds, put Day 2 seeds on the soaking deck in a separate jar at this time.

Day 2 seeds already have a tiny, sprouted tail.

Here are Day 3 seeds between rinses.

DAY 2

Morning: Cover Day 1 (and Day 2) seeds by 2–3 inches of fresh water, swirl them around in the jar aggressively to rinse them, and drain out the water. Place the jar upside-down (or at an upside-down diagonal) back in the cool, shaded area.

Evening: Cover Day 1 (and Day 2) seeds/sprouts by 2–3 inches of fresh water, swirl them around in the jar aggressively to rinse them, and drain out the water. Place the jar upside-down (or at an upside-down diagonal) back in the cool, shaded area.

Note: If you want to sprout more than two jars of seeds, put Day 3 seeds on the soaking deck in a separate jar at this time.

DAY 3

Morning: Cover Day 1 (and Days 2, 3) seeds by 2–3 inches of fresh water, swirl them around in the jar aggressively to rinse them, and drain out the water. Place the jar upside-down (or at an upside-down diagonal) back in the cool, shaded area.

Evening: Cover Day 1 (and Days 2, 3) seeds/sprouts by 2–3 inches of fresh water, swirl them around in the jar aggressively to rinse them, and drain out the water. Place the jar upside-down (or at an upside-down diagonal) back in the cool, shaded area.

Note: If you want to sprout more than three jars of seeds, put Day 4 seeds on the soaking deck in a separate jar at this time.

By Day 4, growth is very noticeable.

By Day 5, just 2 tablespoons of seeds now nearly fill the entire 1-quart glass jar.

DAY 4

Morning: Cover Day 1 (and Days 2, 3, 4) seeds/sprouts by 2–3 inches of fresh water, swirl them around in the jar aggressively to rinse them, and drain out the water. Place the jar upside-down (or at an upside-down diagonal) back in the cool, shaded area.

Evening: Cover Day 1 (and Days 2, 3, 4) seeds/sprouts by 2–3 inches of fresh water, swirl them around in the jar aggressively to rinse them, and drain out the water. Place the jar upside-down (or at an upside-down diagonal) back in the cool, shaded area.

Note: If you want to sprout more than four jars of seeds, put Day 5 seeds on the soaking deck in a separate jar at this time.

DAY 5

Morning: Cover Day 1 (and Days 2, 3, 4, 5) seeds/sprouts by 2–3 inches of fresh water, swirl them around in the jar aggressively to rinse them, and drain out the water. Place the jar upside-down (or at an upside-down diagonal) back in the cool, shaded area.

Evening: Cover Day 1 (and Days 2, 3, 4, 5) seeds/sprouts by 2–3 inches of fresh water, swirl them around in the jar aggressively to rinse them, and drain out the water. Place the jar upside-down (or at an upside-down diagonal) back in the cool, shaded area.

Note: If you want to sprout more than five jars of seeds, put Day 6 seeds on the soaking deck in a separate jar at this time.

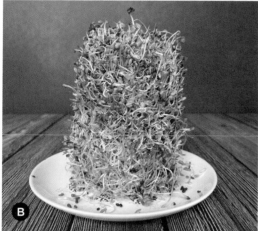

(A) A packed jar of fresh sprouts is ready to harvest on the evening of Day 6.
(B) When your sprouts are ready to harvest, you'll end up with a jar-shaped mass of sprouts.

DAY 6

Morning: Cover Day 1 (and Days 2, 3, 4, 5, 6) seeds/sprouts by 2–3 inches of fresh water, swirl them around in the jar aggressively to rinse them, and drain out the water. Place the jar upside-down (or at an upside-down diagonal) back in the cool, shaded area.

Evening: It is time to harvest your Day 1 sprouts. Empty the sprouts into a colander and rinse several times to get rid of all the seed hulls. They are not poisonous, so you do not have to get them all. Shake dry, and then the sprouts can be eaten raw, cooked in meals, or stored.

Note: To continue the six-day sprouting cycle, simply clean the empty jar and put new sprouting seeds on the soaking deck. Repeat the morning and evening rinse and drain routines for the rest of the jars.

Sprouting Tips

Keep the following things in mind when sprouting:

- **Keep it clean:** Cleanliness is especially important when it comes to sprouting. Start with clean jars and sprouting lids. Use only fresh potable drinking water for rinsing and soaking. Always wash your hands before handling sprouts and seeds. These measures will prevent something else besides sprouts, like bacteria, from growing in your jar. There is a myth that sprouts are dangerous when eaten raw, but it is not true. The headlines we have all seen about people getting sick from eating sprouts at restaurants or grocery stores is due to poor handling and cleaning, not the sprouts themselves.
- **Eat them raw or cooked:** Sprouts can be eaten raw or cooked. I've found that the larger sprouts from beans, peas, and lentils are better for cooking. The smaller ones, such as alfalfa and clover, wilt away too quickly with heat, so I typically eat those raw in salads, on sandwiches, or just by themselves. Note: Kidney bean sprouts should always be cooked.
- **Is that mold?:** Some sprouts in their early stages grow fuzzy white root structures that can resemble mold to the beginner sprouter. It

A shaded kitchen counter corner out of the sun is the perfect spot for sprouting.

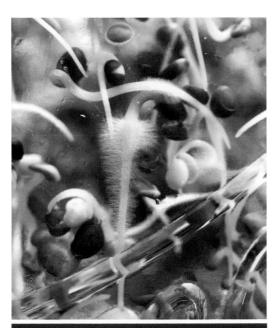

White fuzzy root structures on early-growth sprouts might resemble mold, but they are not. It's perfectly safe to keep sprouting.

ONLINE SPROUTING CLASS

As a bonus for reading this book, I would like to give you a coupon code so that you can take my Online Survival Sprouting Course for free. It is normally $19.99, but if you enter the code READY at checkout, it will be discounted 100 percent for you. In this full video course, I teach my six-day survival sprouting cycle and more. I walk you through each step of the process in my home kitchen and give you a tour of my personal long-term food storage pantry. Get instant access now at www.outdoorcore.com/courses/survival-sprouting-how-to-sprout-greens-long-term-food-storage.

is totally normal and *not* mold. It is simply a part of the plant and will disappear after a couple more days of sprouting.

- **Give them a chlorophyll boost:** Placing your sprouts in a slightly sunny area on the last day of sprouting can green them up. This boost in chlorophyl can have added health benefits such as natural antioxidants.

- **Store your fresh harvest sprouts:** Sprouts will keep for two to three days on the counter or up to one week in sealed containers or zip-top bags in the refrigerator. For long-term food storage, sprouts are best stored in their seed form until needed.

WATER

Water is arguably the single most valuable survival resource for human existence on planet Earth. It is critical to almost every bodily function. Access to fresh drinking water should be at the core of every good long-term preparedness plan, yet it is a category to which far too many people give little thought. In this portion of the book, we will focus on how to source, store, and filter water when your primary source runs dry or is otherwise undrinkable.

Water is heavy and bulky, and storing a lot of it can be cumbersome. The chapters in this part will teach you the proven methods, using various containers, for storing water for five-plus years before needing to drain and refresh. Whether you're storing 1-gallon jugs under your bed or 55-gallon drums in your garage, you can build a buffer of water storage for your peace of mind.

After storage, you'll learn how to identify and implement a renewable source of backup drinking water. You'll learn about open water sources, manual pump wells, well points, and how to implement a rain catchment system for an infinite and passive supply of potable water.

Lastly, you will choose a long-term water filter to keep on hand for an emergency. This will be used to filter and make potable water from any number of sources. I will show you exactly what you need to keep on hand to have confidence that you and your family have access to safe drinking water.

CHAPTER 6

Long-Term Water Storage

FOOD

WATER

HEATING

SANITATION

Few things are more important than water when it comes to human survival. Water is critical to many aspects of sheltering in place, yet few people have long-term water storage or any kind of a water plan in place if the tap stops running or becomes polluted. No amount of food or other preparations will help if your access to water is interrupted, even for just a few days. This chapter will discuss how much water you should have on hand for each person in your household and some critical things to consider when storing it.

The Importance of Water

According to the United States Environmental Protection Agency (EPA.gov/watersense/statistics-and-facts), each American uses an average of 82 gallons of water per day. Not each household. Each American. This is a lot of water!

Most people have no idea how much water they use on any given day. Water is used for drinking, cooking, flushing the toilet, bathing, washing hands, washing dishes, washing clothes, watering the dog, watering plants, watering the garden, watering the lawn, and the list goes on and on. To prepare for a shelter-in-place disaster, we must prioritize our water usage. But even doing that can be tricky, with so many variables at play. At the end of the day, everyone needs to have enough water for drinking, food preparation, and basic hygiene.

I recommend planning on 2 gallons of water per person per day at a bare minimum, which comes out to 56 gallons of water per week for a family of four. That is equivalent to more than ten 5-gallon buckets and over 450 pounds of water for just one week. I use these figures not to overwhelm you but to illustrate that not only is water a big deal for survival, but it is also a big deal (physically) when it comes to storage logistics.

Water is cumbersome, heavy, and takes up a lot of physical storage space. Because of this, you should have two strategies in place. The first strategy revolves around storing water long-term. This chapter and the next two will teach you everything you need to know about doing that as efficiently and safely as possible. Second, because it is just not practical for most people to store more than a few months' worth of water for their family, everyone should have a plan for harvesting more water from renewable sources to supplement the water in long-term storage. Chapter 8 will share some solutions for this.

The average American uses 82 gallons of water each day.

Understanding Chlorine

Before we dig into water storage, I want to touch on chlorine because it is a chemical you hear a lot about when it comes to long-term water storage and purification. But it is also a chemical that few people really understand. In general, most information you read or hear will throw around three different terms for "chlorine," sometimes interchangeably:

- Sodium hypochlorite
- Household bleach
- Calcium hypochlorite

While these can all be used to treat and store water, as a student of survival and preparedness, you need to understand the difference. Understanding this will help you best prepare to use one or all of them in the future.

SODIUM HYPOCHLORITE

Sodium hypochlorite is a liquid form of chlorine. It is a common chemical used in treating swimming pools and even municipal water. Sodium hypochlorite is used to make household bleach, and it has a shelf life of around one year. Even that can be greatly reduced if it is stored in direct sunlight or at high temperatures.

HOUSEHOLD BLEACH

Sodium hypochlorite is diluted to make your run-of-the-mill household bleach, which is normally 5–10 percent sodium hypochlorite. For example, a 6 percent bleach solution can be made from mixing 6 percent sodium hypochlorite and 94 percent water. As you can see, your normal household bleach is not nearly as strong as straight sodium hypochlorite. That is a big deal when it comes to putting these chemicals into your body. "Pool shock" products are like household bleach except stronger, normally around 12.5 percent sodium hypochlorite. Household bleach also has a one-year shelf life that is reduced by storing it in sunlight or at high temperatures.

(A) Clorox brand bleach is a 7.5 percent sodium hypochlorite solution. (B) Calcium hypochlorite tablets and granules are sold in a kit to sanitize (or "shock") well water.

CALCIUM HYPOCHLORITE

Calcium hypochlorite, also known as high test hypochlorite (HTH), comes in dry, white granules and typically contains a chlorine concentration of around 70 percent. It is also commonly sold as a pool shock or well shock product. All my research suggests that calcium hypochlorite has a much longer shelf life than its liquid counterparts. Though sources differ, the average seems to be ten or so years if it is stored in a cool, dry place out of sunlight.

The Role of Chlorine in Long-Term Water Storage

Every household should have a plan when it comes to making questionable water safe to drink. Boiling is an option, but it is very labor- and resource-heavy. Filtering is a great option, and will be discussed in Chapter 9. Using a version of chlorine is a great backup alternative as well.

For years I stocked and rotated a few gallons of household bleach until a friend introduced me to the granular calcium hypochlorite that he used to treat his well water from time to time. Now I store a small kit of this instead. Calcium hypochlorite can be dissolved in water to make a 5 percent chlorine solution like household bleach. This solution can then be used to disinfect questionable water.

In 2005, the United States Army put out a bulletin called *Sanitary Control and Surveillance of Field Water Supplies*. It includes a chart that details the volume of dry HTH required to make a 5 percent bleach solution. The 1-gallon calculation is the one we at the household level are most interested in. Simply mix 1 gallon of water with ½ cup of dry granular HTH to make a 5 percent bleach solution. Note that this is *not* drinking water! This is a solution used to sanitize drinking water. This is essentially the same as household bleach and will thus have a shelf life of one year. This solution can then be used to disinfect hundreds of gallons of water if needed.

According to the Centers for Disease Control and Prevention (CDC), a 5–9 percent concentration of chlorine solution can be used in the following proportions to disinfect water for drinking:

- 2 drops of 5 percent solution for 1 liter of water
- 8 drops of 5 percent solution for 1 gallon of water
- 40 drops of 5 percent solution for 5 gallons of water

After stirring in the 5 percent solution, the mixture should be left to sit for 30 minutes before drinking. The CDC also notes that if the water is cloudy, murky, colored, or very cold, then the number of drops of 5 percent solution should be doubled.

It is important to note that HTH is very corrosive and does not play well with others. Because of this, it is important to store HTH by itself in its original container in a cool, dry area. Do not store HTH in a metal container or with other chemicals unless you want to see some fireworks.

Important Considerations

The next two chapters will cover many storage containers and options, including the popular 55-gallon plastic drum and some other very interesting options, such as the WaterBrick system. But before that, it is important to cover a few basics. First, we'll talk about the ideal water storage conditions.

In a perfect world, water would be stored long-term in a cool, dry place out of the sunlight and with easy daily access for using, draining, or refilling. It would also be nice if the water, especially in large containers, was stored on a concrete platform that is out of plain sight so as not to advertise long-term water storage to passersby. But a perfect world is rarely reality, and we all must simply do the best we can to cross as many of those ideal circumstances off the list. The most important ones to prioritize are listed here.

OUT OF DIRECT SUNLIGHT

Direct sunlight promotes algae growth. Algae will not kill you and can be filtered out, but it would be best to avoid it altogether. One easy way to do this is to use opaque containers, such as solid blue or black plastic containers, or to cover your storage containers with tarps. While I was training in survival skills with the Paipai people in Baja California, Mexico, I noticed that all their drinking water was stored in large black tanks. This was to help prevent algae growth in the hot desert sun.

ON A SOLID SURFACE ON GROUND LEVEL

Large containers can weigh hundreds of pounds, so falling or toppling is a dangerous possibility. And, if they fall and burst open in the house, it can create an entirely new set of problems, such as

This black gravity-fed water storage container, which sat above the house, supplied water to my hosts in Mexico for months at a time. Large above-ground water containers like this can be extremely dangerous if not supported and secured properly.

mold—not to mention the loss of water. Be sure to consider the weight of larger containers; a 55-gallon drum of water weighs almost 500 pounds! As you will see later, I have a 305-gallon water storage tank in my garage that weighs over 2,500 pounds. This could collapse even the best-built floor. So you definitely want to store such large containers on solid ground.

EASY ACCESS

Small containers can be tucked away, but when it comes to filling large immovable containers of water, it is important to think about access. You may need to access these containers multiple times a day in a shelter-in-place scenario. You may also need to drain them in a few years to replace the water. Thinking through access before you turn on the hose and start filling is a really good idea. When I first bought my 55-gallon drums, I placed them where I thought I wanted them while they were still empty and left them there for a couple of weeks. I ultimately found that they were in the way and decided to move them. I am glad I waited to fill them up!

How Long Will Water Store?

This is the most common question I get about long-term water storage, and is another topic that comes with many mixed opinions. I used to store all my water for one year. Each year I would empty and replace my water storage. These days I store my water for five years and will likely push that to ten years soon because of all the occasions I've opened a storage container of water after five years and found it to be perfectly fine. I will cover the details of storing water in the next two chapters. For now, you should understand the following.

COMMERCIALLY PURCHASED OR TAP WATER

Any commercially bought water (bottled water) or tap water will store for at least five years without needing any additional chemicals. There seems to be enough residual chlorine in tap water to keep it from going bad. However, I still add a 5 percent chlorine solution to my stored water for good measure. I use the same amount for storage as I do in the dosages I provided earlier for water disinfection from the CDC. I ramped up the calculations to accommodate 55-gallon drums, and it comes to roughly 5 teaspoons of 5–9 percent chlorine solution. For the smaller containers I just use the recommended number of drops.

WELL WATER OR NATURALLY SOURCED WATER

For well water, groundwater, rainwater, or water harvested from any other natural source, I would recommend adding the required disinfection dose of 5 percent chlorine solution at the time of storage.

FILTERING

Every household should have at least one disaster survival water filter. Chapter 9 will show you the best options. I plan on filtering all my stored water through my disaster water filter. Even if the stored water grows bacteria or algae, leaches plastic, or goes bad in some other way, it does not matter. My water filter will make it safe to drink again. Water storage is more about having water available. Your water filter can make it safe to drink.

FOOD
WATER
HEATING
SANITATION

CHAPTER 7

Water Storage Containers

This chapter will save you time and money by giving you a quick list of available water storage containers to choose from. No experimenting, no testing, and no buying containers that will not work. I have done all of that research for you over the years. All you have to do is choose one or more of the options I detail in this chapter and start filling!

Small Storage Containers

For the purposes of this book, I consider small storage containers to be anything that holds 2 gallons or less. An assortment of small containers is great because they can be creatively tucked just about anywhere in your home, even if you are limited on space. Following is a discussion of a few options to consider when it comes to small containers.

STORE-BOUGHT BOTTLED WATER

Store-bought bottled water in virtually any size is a quick, safe, worry-free, and easy small-container water storage option. You can be assured the water inside is safe to drink and will store for an exceptionally long time. I have no problem with storing store-bought water for five years, especially when running it through my Big Berkey water filter (detailed in Chapter 9) before drinking.

I have a love-hate relationship with the smaller case-packed bottled water. On the one hand, I hate those plastic bottles because they are horrible for the environment. On the other hand, it is hard to deny how well a few cases of those bottles stack in a storage closet or garage. They are certainly a quick, easy, and inexpensive small-scale water storage solution.

The larger containers of store-bought water, such as 1-gallon jugs, are more difficult to store because they do not stack well. A solution to this is a thin piece of plywood or similar material in between single-stack layers of bottles. When you stack them this way, you can build a remarkably sturdy block of water that could easily be used as a piece of furniture or even a work bench. Three layers tall of 1-gallon jugs with circle-cut plywood in between makes a perfect instant end table when covered with a piece of fabric. I have "false floors" of 1-gallon jugs of store-bought water in several of my closets and armoires using this technique. You lose very little closet space at the bottom and retain most, if not all, of the functionality.

REPURPOSED PLASTIC BOTTLES

Repurposing plastic bottles such as 2-liter pop bottles for water storage is a common practice within the preparedness community. There was a time that I did this and recommended it. Plastic 2-liter bottles are made from polyethylene terephthalate (also called PET or PETE), which is approved by the United States Food and Drug Administration (FDA) for use in packaging drinks and food. It does not contain bisphenol A (BPA) or phthalates (plasticizers).

Even though repurposed 2-liters are safe for storing water, I no longer do it. I now store water only in repurposed bottles that originally contained water. I have discovered that finding bottles that once held water (say, from friends and family) is just as easy these days as finding 2-liter bottles that contained something else, such as soda. Using repurposed water bottles does not come with the typical compromises and drawbacks. These include having to thoroughly wash out sugary residue, flavorings, or syrups from the bottles and having your stored water still taste like whatever was in the bottle before it. Plastic is porous and absorbs the flavor and other micro-ingredients of whatever is stored inside it. No matter how much you wash the bottle, you will never get all of that residue out of the plastic, and it will leach

(A) Two layers of plastic 1-gallon jugs stacked with wood in between are ready to be covered in fabric to make an instant end table. (B) This end table is hiding 14 gallons of long-term water storage.

into your water over time. Using upcycled 2-liter pop bottles sounds good until you do it. There are plenty of water bottles out there to repurpose if you want to go that route.

As a side note, if you do decide to repurpose plastic bottles for water storage, do not use containers that once stored milk. The leaching of potential milk proteins can create an ideal environment for dangerous bacterial growth in your water.

Medium Storage Containers

I consider medium-sized containers to be those that hold 2–10 gallons of water. Water weighs 8.34 pounds per gallon, so handling these containers starts to get a little cumbersome once you get into the 5-gallon range (41.64 pounds). Even so, there are several good commercially available options on the market for this size range. I have listed the ones you may want to consider for your own storage here.

WATERBRICK

The WaterBrick comes in 3.5-gallon and 1.6-gallon sizes. This is an incredibly unique water storage option for several reasons. First, unlike many medium-sized container options, the WaterBrick is stackable. The interlocking design allows you to safely cross stack each container in a closet, basement, or garage. A ¾-inch PVC pipe can be inserted through the internal columns for safter stacking. The WaterBrick is also compatible with the FoodBrick (discussed in Chapter 3); they can be stacked together for a true long-term storage system. The resin used in these containers meets FDA standards and is BPA-free, making them safe for food and water. Each WaterBrick has the option for a steel handle, which makes this container easy to move and handle. These would be ideal containers to toss into a bug out vehicle in a hurry. At the time of this writing, a two-pack of 3.5-gallon Water-Bricks is available at WaterBrick.org for about $35.

4.5-GALLON WATER JUG BY MIDWEST CAN

Midwest Can is an Illinois-based manufacturer of plastic fuel cans. They also make a 4.5-gallon BPA-free water jug. This seems to be one of the best-priced water jugs on the market. They list various retailers

WaterBricks and FoodBricks have an interlocking design for safe and easy stacking.

(A) This 3.5-gallon WaterBrick is made in the USA. (B) This 4.5-gallon water jug is made by Midwest Can. (C) This 7-gallon Aqua-Tainer is made by Canada-based Reliance.

on their website (MidwestCan.com). At the time of this writing, you can also buy them online from True Value hardware stores (TrueValue .com) for around $12 and have them shipped free to your local store. These aren't recommended for stacking, and you will need to keep them out of the sun because they are clear, but they are definitely an option for long-term water storage in the 5-gallon range.

RELIANCE PRODUCTS AQUA-TAINER

If you search the Internet for water storage containers for more than 30 seconds you will likely come across the 7-gallon Aqua-Tainer by Reliance of Canada (RelianceOutdoors.com). This has been a long-time favorite water container for campers and outdoor enthusiasts. Along with several similar containers that Reliance makes, it is also well suited for long-term water storage at home. The Aqua-Tainer is BPA-free and includes a hideaway spigot that reverses into the opening for easy storage. The molded handle makes this an option for tossing in the car for a camping trip or bug out if needed. If 7 gallons seems too cumbersome, they also make a 4-gallon version.

55-Gallon Plastic Drums

When it comes to large long-term water storage containers, the 55-gallon plastic drum is the most popular, affordable, and available. It is roughly 24 inches in diameter by 36 inches tall and weighs just over 450 pounds when full. These are ideal for storing large volumes of water in the garage, basement, barn, or outbuilding, or along the side of the house. In addition to several smaller containers, I have six 55-gallon drums, which together store roughly 330 gallons of water. I use these to form the base of a workbench in my garage. When using 55-gallon drums for water storage, there are some important things you need to know.

WEIGHT AND SIZE

At over 450 pounds when full, 55-gallon drums are extremely heavy and almost impossible to move without emptying. For this reason, it is critical they be filled in an area with a solid foundation that can

Food-grade 55-gallon plastic drums are very popular large water storage containers.

support the weight. Concrete slabs in the garage or basement or solid ground outside or in a barn are ideal. I do not recommend filling these drums on an upper story or balcony. It is also especially important that they are stable. A toppling 55-gallon drum of water is extremely dangerous and can potentially flood an area if it breaks open. This results in not only water loss and property damage, but also in potential mold issues in a shelter-in-place scenario where power might not be available. The falling weight from a 55-gallon drum could also seriously injure someone.

FOOD GRADE ONLY

There are many different types of plastic drums on the market. Some are food grade and some are not. The seller should always make this distinction by indicating that the drum is FDA compliant or "food grade." Food-grade drums are made from resins that are deemed safe by the FDA, and although you will likely be filtering all stored water (discussed in Chapter 9) before use, it is a good idea to start with food-grade drums.

NEW VERSUS USED

In your quest to save money, you may be tempted to purchase used 55-gallon drums, and some sources even recommend this. I do not. I use and suggest using only new plastic drums for several reasons. First, plastic is porous on the microscopic level. The previously stored liquid in these drums absorbs into the plastic walls. These trace amounts of liquid and chemicals can then leach into the water stored in the drum. If the previously stored liquid is a food product, such as flavoring syrup for a soda company, this will not harm you. But I can promise that your water will taste like whatever was in it before. I personally do not want to be using slightly grape-flavored water to make my beans and rice, do you? On a more serious note, even if a seller tells you that the previously stored liquid was a food product, what if it was not? What if it was shampoo, a soap ingredient, or other chemical? The leaching of anything like this into your water supply could be downright dangerous. The few dollars of savings is simply not worth the risk.

BUNG HOLES, BUNG NUTS, AND A BUNG WRENCH

Apparently, a bung hole is not just a name to call your little brother, like I did growing up. All standard plastic 55-gallon drums have two openings on top, called bung holes. Both have screw-in caps, called bung nuts. Usually one bung nut has a fine thread and one has a coarse thread. The top of each threaded bung nut has a recessed cross shape. A special tool, called a bung wrench, is used to unscrew and tighten the bung nuts. You will want to pick up a bung wrench if you decide to use 55-gallon drums for water storage. You can find the one I use at the online resource page for this book. I also keep a few extra fine- and coarse-thread bung nuts on hand just in case I lose one of the originals.

You will need a specially designed bung wrench to loosen and tighten the cross-shaped bung nuts in a 55-gallon drum.

CLEAN FOUNDATION

As mentioned, the plastic walls of 55-gallon drums can leach chemicals from whatever was stored inside. But this can also happen from what is *outside* the drum. For this reason, you want to store your drums on clean surfaces. Clean concrete, wood, and gravel are all good options. If in doubt, place them on a base of 2 × 4-inch lumber. Do not store them in areas where gas, oil, fertilizer, lawn chemicals, pesticides, or other pollutants may be spilled or pool around the bottoms.

LOCATION, LOCATION, LOCATION

Filling 55-gallon drums with water is a commitment. Once they are full, they are exceedingly difficult to relocate. You will need to empty out the water to move them. For this reason, I encourage you to sleep on their location for a few days before committing. Go ahead and place them, empty, where you think you will want them. Then, just go on with your life for a few days and make sure the location is going to make sense. You may decide they are in the way, inconvenient, or an eyesore. Give yourself some time to make sure you are ready for them to be immovable.

In addition, there are two points you need to consider about the location of your large water storage containers. First, imagine you will need to harvest water from them five to ten times a day. Are they in a convenient enough spot for repeated daily use? Second, if the water is not consumed, you will eventually need to empty the drums to replace the water. Are they in a convenient spot for empty-ing? Emptying, as you'll learn later in this chapter, is typically done using a manual barrel pump. You can pump into smaller containers and carry the water away, or you can pump to start a drainage flow and drain through a hose into your yard or garden. Either way, you want to make sure both are possible and practical before you fill the drums with 55 gallons of water.

FREEZE WARNING

Yes, the water in large storage containers can freeze. If you live in a four-season environment, this is an important consideration. In early 2021, even Texas saw record-low spring temperatures that froze water pipes inside homes. If there is even a remote chance of extended time below freezing, you may want to reconsider your storage location.

Preparation and Filling for Long-Term Storage

Filling drums for long-term storage isn't rocket science, but there are a few important notes I'd like to mention for both safety and efficiency.

STEP 1
Cleaning Process

Once you have picked out a good location, it is time to prepare your drums for filling. I recommend thoroughly rinsing them out even though you will be filtering any water that you use from them. The inside has a strong smell of resin, and there is likely some residue, dust, and particles still inside from production, storage, and/or travel. I always take the extra step to wash my drums first before I add my drinking water. Following is my simple three-step process for doing this.

1. Bring your drum out into the yard and pour in around 4 gallons of fresh water. Adding a few squirts of dish soap is optional; note that it will take several extra rinses to get it all out.

2. Tighten both bung nuts and turn the drum on its side. Then, aggressively roll the drum back and forth to make sure the water rinses off all inner surfaces. Do this for a few minutes.

3. There is a recessed grip on one side of the bottom that makes it easy to tilt the drum and pour out the water. Once you have done this, the drum is ready to fill with fresh water for storage.

STEP 2-A

STEP 2-B

STEP 2

Filling Process

Filling is pretty self-explanatory.

1. Start by placing the drum in your chosen final location.
2. Fill the drum halfway with fresh water from a hose. If you are using any chemicals for storage (see Chapter 6), add those now. This is when I add 5 teaspoons of 5–9 percent chlorine solution.
3. Fill the remainder to within a couple inches of the top.
4. Tighten both bung nuts with your bung wrench.
5. Use a permanent marker to write the date of storage and any chemicals used on the top or side of the drum. You could also use labels or duct tape instead of writing directly on the drum.

How to Use a Drum Siphon

There are several options on the market for pumping water out of your drum when the time comes for drinking or draining. There are manual pumps, electric pumps, and even battery-operated pumps. I recommend the simplest and least expensive option of them all: a simple manual drum siphon.

A 55-gallon drum siphon can be purchased online for around $30. You can find the ones I recommend at the online resource for this book. The ones made specifically for 55-gallon plastic drums have a long tube that reaches the bottom of the drum and a housing that screws into the fine-threaded bung hole. Following are the steps for using one.

STEP 1
Inserting the Siphon Tube

Insert the long, fixed siphon tube into the bung hole with the fine threads, then securely screw in the red siphon housing.

STEP 2
Tightening the Air Valve

There is a little screw knob on the very top of the housing. This is an air valve that must be closed before the siphon will work. Tighten this until it stops.

STEP 3

Connecting to the Smaller Container

Place your flexible siphon hose in a smaller container. In this case I am using a 3.5-gallon WaterBrick to transport water from my 55-gallon drum.

STEP 4

Getting the Pump Going

Start pumping the siphon pump in an up-and-down motion. It will take only a few pumps for water to start flowing. Once the flexible hose is full, the pump will continue to draw water on its own without the need for pumping.

To stop the flow of water when the smaller container is full, loosen the air valve knob on the top of the pump. It is fine to leave the pump installed between siphons as you ready your next small container.

STEP 3

STEP 4

Water Storage Tanks

Millions of people around the globe get all their fresh drinking water delivered by truck to large water storage tanks. There are also many industrial and farm uses for large water storage tanks. If you have the space, such as a larger garage, barn, or available outdoor area, water storage tanks much larger than 55-gallon drums are available for your consideration. For example, I bought a 305-gallon emergency water tank from National Tank Outlet (NTOTank.com). I was able to catch it on sale for just over $300 plus freight, which is an incredible buy.

National Tank Outlet has dozens of BPA-free water storage tanks to choose from in sizes ranging from 100 gallons to as large as you would ever need. I store my 305-gallon tank in the corner of my garage. The water spigot is low on the tank, so I have the tank raised

This 305-gallon water storage tank sits in the corner of my garage.

on an 18-inch-tall platform made from cement cinder blocks to support the weight (over 2,500 pounds when filled). I installed an outlet valve that has a garden hose adapter (available as an add-on purchase from National Tank Outlet). This allows me to easily fill various-sized smaller containers or run a hose outside to drain the tank when that time comes.

FOOD

WATER

HEATING

SANITATION

CHAPTER 8

Renewable Water Sources

"Renewable water source" simply means a source of water that is not permanently depleted when used. If your long-term storage strategy and timeline does not extend beyond a few months, establishing a renewable water source may not be a priority for you. I personally never felt like my storage preps were complete without one. Luckily, there are options that will work for almost anyone in any situation. This chapter will review the renewable water sources that are the most practical for the average household.

Open Water Sources

The easiest and most accessible renewable water sources are naturally occurring: creeks, rivers, streams, and ponds. These were the original water supply for our native ancestors. Unfortunately, many of our open water sources these days are laced with pollutants from industry, pesticides, trash, fertilizers, lawn chemicals, sewage, roadways, vehicle chemicals, and more. This is especially true with water sources located within cities and suburbs. Even seemingly clean waterways that meander through the countryside are subject to large amounts of runoff farming chemicals, fertilizers, herbicides, pesticides, and more.

In addition to commercial chemicals, all open water sources can also be exposed to microbiological threats, such as protozoan cysts, bacteria, and viruses. Some of the most common ones we hear about are giardia, cryptosporidium, *E. coli*, rotavirus, norovirus, hepatitis A, and *Salmonella*. The primary source for these biological threats is the feces from an infected animal or human. Drinking water infected with these various microscopic parasites is the leading cause of death in the world, claiming millions of lives each year—mostly in nations where sewage control and sanitation measures are below standard. Open water sources are especially vulnerable during large-scale disasters such as earthquakes and floods that may cause sewage pipes to break or septic containments to overflow. It is well known that raw sewage pours into open waterways during heavy rains in many of America's largest cities. Dead livestock, pets, and other animals in waterways can also become a contamination issue during certain types of disasters. Furthermore, destroyed gas lines, businesses, or other industrial areas can cause a wide variety of pollutants to temporarily mix with open water sources.

Bringing water to a rolling boil will kill all biological parasites, but it will not remove chemicals, heavy metals, or other industrial pollutants. For this reason, a reliable water filter should be a part of everyone's disaster preparedness plan. Chapter 9 will discuss your best filter options. For now, just know that open water sources can be a viable option under the right circumstances.

Rain Harvesting

I consider rain harvesting to be a required piece of every home disaster water plan. When most people think about rain harvesting, they think of expensive, hard-to-install, and unsightly pipes and tanks. This could not be further from the truth. If you have a roof of any kind with a gutter, I will teach you how to install an unobtrusive 55-gallon rain barrel in 20 minutes or less with a $50 do-it-yourself kit. But first, it is important to understand a few things:

- Rain harvesting makes sense for almost everyone. Unless you live in an extremely arid climate that receives almost zero rainfall, installing a rain barrel is a worthwhile investment. For the small amount of time and money you will spend getting one installed, the reward is an almost effortless renewable source of emergency drinking water. This water can also be used for pets, gardening, washing, or bathing.
- Rainwater is safe to drink without filtering or purification. However, as it falls on your roof and makes its way into the rain barrel, it picks up debris. Because of this, rain barrel water should be considered wild water that needs to be properly filtered or purified to make it safe to drink. I will discuss the filters you need to consider for this step in Chapter 9.
- Believe it or not, there are laws in some states that prohibit or restrict homeowners from harvesting rainwater from their own roofs. Some homeowners' associations may also have rules in place that prohibit rain barrels. You will want to check to make sure before you install a rain barrel. Otherwise, a citation of some kind might make its way into your mailbox. (Or you can just move to a place with fewer restrictions on your personal freedoms.)
- I have used numerous types of rain barrels over the years and have been most happy with a 55-gallon plastic drum conversion. They are not necessarily the most aesthetically pleasing of rain barrels, but I have found them to be durable, cost effective, and functional. These standard 55-gallon blue drums

IT ADDS UP

For every inch of rain that falls on a 1,000-square-foot roof, you can expect to be able to collect 600 gallons of rainwater! Now that is a serious return on investment.

Rain barrels are hooked up to gutter downspouts like this one to collect rainwater that falls on a roof's large surface area.

can be painted to match your home if desired. The key to doing so is prepping the surface of the drum by roughing it up with some sandpaper. The factory finish of these drums has an almost waxy residue that the sandpaper treatment removes. I suggest a spray paint that is made for outdoor use and that bonds to plastic. Plan on using at least two full cans to coat one 55-gallon drum.

Before starting, you will need to pick up some parts to convert your plastic drum into a rain barrel. The kit I recommend includes everything you need, including the drill bits and hole saws. It's called the EarthMinded DIY Rain Barrel Diverter and Parts Kit. I include links to it at the online resource page for this book. It's made to work with the most common rectangular downspouts, which are 2 × 3 inches or 3 × 4 inches, but you can buy extra pieces to make it work with round downspouts. The good news is that you can use this kit with virtually any size drum or container. You do not have to use a full-sized 55-gallon drum; 15- or 30-gallon drums work equally as well.

(A) Before painting a 55-gallon plastic drum, lightly sand the drum with sandpaper. (B) After sanding your plastic drum, use an outdoor spray paint that bonds to plastic to coat the drum. Expect to use two full cans.

Installing a Drum Rain Barrel and Gutter Diverter Kit

The instructions included with the kit are very thorough, but here are the basic steps for setting up your own 55-gallon drum rain barrel at home.

STEP 1

Planning for the Platform

The inside edge of your rain barrel must be within 6–28 inches from the outside edge of the downspout. This is the minimum and maximum distance the fill hose connecting the barrel to the downspout will shrink and expand. Before prepping your platform, place your drum near the downspout and figure out a nice place for it that meets those dimensions. You may find that uneven ground, plants, rocks, or other obstructions make some downspouts unusable for rain barrels. It is better to discover this *before* prepping your barrel platform. A solid platform serves two purposes.

1. First, a full 55-gallon drum weighs almost 500 pounds. A well-prepared platform ensures your drum will not tip or fall over.
2. Second, a platform should lift your rain barrel off the ground. Most spigots are positioned toward the bottom of the rain barrel, which can be very inconvenient. A low spigot makes filling containers, such as buckets, difficult. Raising your rain barrel at least 8 inches also helps increase water pressure for watering raised beds, planters, or gardens nearby. The higher your rain barrel, the more water pressure you will have.

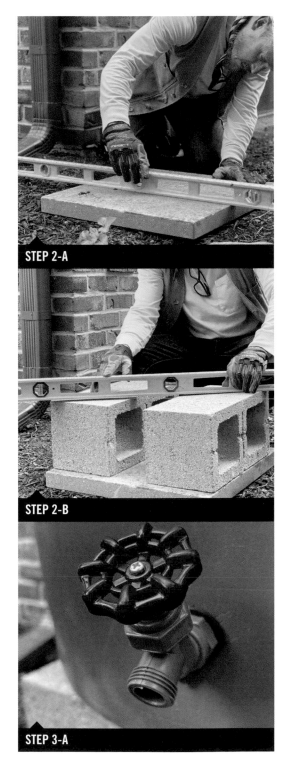

STEP 2-A

STEP 2-B

STEP 3-A

STEP 2

Building the Platform

I build my rain barrel platform in three stages:

1. I prep the ground under where the rain barrel will be with a thick layer of mulch. Mulch helps absorb any excess water that might come from the barrel or spigot during use.
2. I put a layer of solid concrete pavers on the mulch to create a nice level platform. This platform needs to be a minimum of 24 inches square and as level as you can get it.
3. I use two concrete 8 × 16-inch cinder blocks to create a platform that is at least 8 inches off the ground. I find this height provides decent water pressure and allows me to fill most small containers.

STEP 3

Installing the Spigot

The front spigot is what you will use to drain the water from your drum. The kit includes everything you will need to install it: a 1¼-inch hole saw, a rubber gasket, and the spigot itself. Installing the spigot 3–5 inches from the bottom is the perfect height. This is just above the curve of the drum's bottom edge along the flat face. You don't want to install the spigot too high because you won't be able to access the water below it without tipping the drum, which is a real hassle. The few inches below the spigot allows space in the drum for

STEP 3-B

STEP 4-A

STEP 4-B

sediment and ensures you'll be draining relatively clean water without clogging your spigot. Installation is as simple as drilling a hole, inserting the rubber gasket, and screwing in the spigot.

STEP 4

Installing the Fill Hose Gasket

The fill hose gasket is where the fill hose connects to the top of the drum. With your spigot facing the direction you need it, you want the center of your fill hose gasket to be 3–5 inches down from the top of the barrel and located in a place that allows the fill hose to have a nice straight, horizontal path from the downspout. To install it, simply drill a hole using the included 1½-inch hole saw and insert the rubber seal.

STEP 5

Installing the FlexiFit Diverter

The FlexiFit diverter is a specially shaped rubber piece that inserts into the gutter downspout to divert water into the fill hose. But when the rain barrel is full, the FlexiFit diverter allows water to pass through and out the downspout like normal. It is a pretty nifty little invention, but placement on the downspout is key. For closed 55-gallon drums like the one shown here, you want to drill a hole in the downspout at the same level as the top rim of your drum, or slightly higher. I typically lay a level across the top of my barrel and make a mark on the underside on the downspout. Next, measure and mark the center of the downspout at this spot to drill your

$2\frac{1}{8}$-inch hole using the included hole saw. For 2 × 3-inch gutters, you will drill this hole on the wider 3-inch side. But for 3 × 4-inch gutters, you will drill this hole on the narrower 3-inch side. Once the hole is drilled, the FlexiFit diverter is simply inserted and secured to the downspout using two self-tapping screws.

STEP 6

STEP 6

Connecting the Drum

The last step is to insert the fill hose at each end—one into the FlexiFit diverter on the downspout and the other into the fill hose gasket on the upper rim of the drum. Now you will be ready for rain to passively provide a renewable source of survival water for bathing, washing, gardening, or drinking. Note that multiple 55-gallon drums can be daisy-chained together using more fill hose seals and fill hoses. Multiple passive rain harvesting drums could be a very interesting source of survival water if you have the space. These extra parts are available directly from EarthMinded (EarthMinded RainBarrels.com).

Don't forget that even though rainwater is perfectly safe to drink without filtering or purification, what is on your roof and in your gutters may not be. Any water you intend to drink from your rain barrel will need to be filtered and/or purified. The next chapter will detail the filter you need to have as a part of your long-term water strategy.

Manual Well Pumps

An existing water well on your property, whether being used currently or not, is an ideal backup shelter-in-place renewable water source that should not be ignored. The hard and expensive work of drilling or digging has already been done.

Most private water wells these days have an electric pump. Electric pumps, of course, are dependent on electricity. Especially if a well is your main water source, that presents a serious problem. The solution, assuming no electric backup power source is available, is a hand-operated well pump. Before buying one, there are some important details you need to know to determine which pump is right for your circumstances.

SHALLOW VERSUS DEEP PUMPS

Shallow well pumps can lift water from a depth of 20–25 feet. In contrast, some deep well pumps can push water up from 300-plus feet beneath the surface. You can use a deep well pump for any well depth, but you cannot use a shallow well pump for wells with a water depth of much more than 25 feet. The depth of your well will be one of the first determining factors regarding which type of pump to purchase.

Measuring your well depth is quite simple. First, tie a heavy metal bolt or nut onto the end of a roll of cotton butcher's twine. Then, lower it into the top of your well casing and listen carefully for the sound it makes when it splashes into the water. Use a marker to mark the spot on your twine at this point, then pull the twine out of the well. Measure from the bolt end to your mark to find the depth to the top of your water level. It is important to note that water levels can fluctuate depending on the season.

DIAMETER OF WELL CASING

All manual pumps have a drop pipe that slides down into the well casing and submerses into your well water underground. The pump pulls or pushes the water through this pipe to get to the surface. The diameter of the well casing is therefore an important factor in the style of pump you will be able to use.

If your well has just a well casing with no wiring, existing pump, or T-junctions, then it is likely that any style of hand pump and drop pipe will work fine. However, it is very possible you will already have an existing submersible pump or at least some remaining pipes (and wires) within the first 5 feet of your well casing that are already connected to your house (or were at one time). This added hardware can be a problem for some manual pump drop pipes, especially with well casings like mine that are only 4 inches in diameter. A well casing with a diameter of 6 inches or more will give more room for drop pipes and typically are not a problem.

My recommendation is to ask the manual pump manufacturer you are considering for the diameter of their drop pipe. Then, before purchasing the pump, go to your local hardware store and buy 10 feet of pipe in the same style and diameter of the manufacturer you are considering. This way you can test to make sure you will be able to insert the drop pipe past the first 6 or so feet, where most obstacles are going to be within the well.

My well casing is only 4 inches in diameter. With existing obstacles already in the casing, it does not leave much extra room for inserting a manual pump drop pipe.

Manual Pump Recommendations

There are too many manufacturers of manual pumps to cover them all in this book. Following, I have listed several brands and sources that I am most familiar with. These will help you cut through the clutter if you're looking for a manual pump of your own.

SIMPLE PUMP

Simple Pump (SimplePump.com) is the Cadillac of hand pumps. It is made from stainless steel and can push water up from 325-plus feet. They offer deep and shallow well pump options and also have solar capabilities. You can expect to pay $1,400 or more for one of their deep well pumps, but this is a nice-quality pump that will last for years. The biggest consideration with this pump is whether you can fit the pump cylinder and drop pipe into your existing well casing and past any obstructions that may already be there. In Indiana, where I live, most well casings are 4 inches in diameter. I am not able to install this style of pump because there is not enough room for me to slide the drop pipe down past the existing piping toward the top of my well. If I could, I would have this pump installed on our well.

This stainless steel manual pump by Simple Pump can pump water up from 325-plus feet. It can also be used to pump into your existing pressure tank.

FLOJAK EARTHSTRAW

The EarthStraw, available at Flojak.com, is the manual pump I have installed as a backup on the well at my home. These manual pumps cost $400 or more depending on the depth of your well and drop tube needed. This is the only style of pump that I could fit into my existing 4-inch well casing. It has a ⅞-inch flexible tube that will work with just about any casing. It also has several mounting options that will accommodate just about any circumstance. This is an extremely easy manual pump to install and takes only about 30 minutes from start to finish. It is a great option for tight well casings and can pump water up from about 125 feet.

LEHMAN'S

Lehman's (Lehmans.com) is a brand that helps you lead a simpler life. They sell online but also have an impressive brick-and-mortar location in Ohio. They stock a variety of both deep and shallow well manual pumps that are worth your consideration. Lehman's has been family owned and operated since 1955 and has a good handle on which pumps are worth stocking. They have done most of the due diligence for you.

The EarthStraw manual pump by Flojak has a $7/8$-inch flexible drop tube that will slide into almost any size well casing and alongside existing pump hardware.

Driving Your Own Well Point

If you do not have an existing drilled water well, drilling one is awfully expensive—especially as a survival backup. However, there is a less expensive alternative that few people know about. It is called a driven well point.

A driven well point is a small-diameter (usually 2 inches or less) shallow well that you drive into the ground yourself with a sledgehammer or weighted post driver. It will work only in areas where the water table is roughly 30 feet or higher—any more, and it becomes exceedingly difficult to drive a well point that deep. The type of ground is also a factor. Sandy soil is best, whereas hard, compact clay can be difficult. Rocks or underground boulders can also stop a well point in its tracks. If it sounds like driving a well point is a gamble, you're

FINDING WATER TABLES

The US Geological Society has offices in every state, and they may be able to help you determine what the water table is in your area. Find your local office here: USGS.gov/connect/locations.

These are the materials needed to drive and set up your own well point.

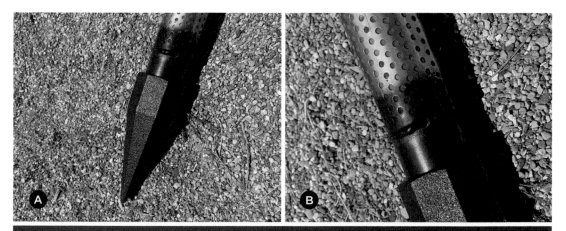

(A) The tip of the well point is a hard, sharp spear for piercing the ground with each whack of the sledgehammer or post driver. (B) The wall of the well point is made with holes and mesh to allow groundwater to seep into the well tube.

right. There are no guarantees, but with a little research and homework you can make a solid educated guess, especially if you know the layout and geology of your property.

A driven well point is made up of a few components. First is the well point itself, which is essentially a cylindrical screen with a sharp tip. The well point is attached to a 1¼- or 2-inch galvanized pipe and is driven into the ground using a post hole driver. Additional lengths of pipe are attached using specialized couplings as the point is driven into the ground. A drive cap is threaded onto the top pipe to protect the threads while driving and is removed when the next piece of pipe is added. Once the water table is reached, the screen on the well point allows water to seep into the pipe. Then a shallow well pump is attached to the top of the pipe at the surface, and water can be pumped out for use. It is a slick do-it-yourself system that can be a great option if you live in an area that meets the criteria.

Following is the step-by-step process for driving your own well point. I use a well point in the campground at my training facility (WillowHavenOutdoor.com) as a source of wash water for campers.

STEP 1

STEP 2

Attaching the Well Point and Pipe

Start by attaching your well point to the first 60-inch length of galvanized pipe with a coupling. I use a 1¼-inch coupling. Be sure to cover all threads with a good pipe joint compound to create a tight seal before joining. Tighten snugly using a pipe wrench.

Digging a Starter Hole

Dig a hole 3–4 feet deep at the location you have chosen (based on research and best guesses) with a post hole digger. This gives you a head start to drive your well point. I like to place my well point in the hole and pack the dirt back in around it. This helps keep the pipe straight as I start driving.

STEP 3

STEP 4

STEP 3

Attaching the Drive Cap

Be sure to screw the drive cap onto the top of the pipe before you start driving. A drive cap is critical so you don't damage the pipe threads while pounding into the ground.

STEP 4

Driving the Well Point Into the Ground

Using a post driver (and possibly a stepladder or chair), drive the well point into the ground. Stop when the pipe is sticking out about 1 foot from the ground. In the photo, I am using a 6-pound post driver to pound 25 feet of galvanized well pipe into the ground, ½ inch at a time.

STEP 5

Attaching More Pipe

Attach a new length of 60-inch galvanized pipe using a coupling, two pipe wrenches, and some joint compound.

STEP 6

Finish Driving the Well Point

Continue driving and keep your fingers crossed. Your well point will need to be completely submersed beneath the water table, or it will suck air. It is a good idea to drive it a couple of feet deeper to account for seasonal water fluctuations. In the photo, I'm standing on a stump to reach the top of a new length of pipe. You could also stand on a stepladder or chair.

STEP 7-A

STEP 7-B

Attaching the Cast Iron Hand Pump

Once the driving is done, it's time to attach your shallow well hand pump. Most of these screw right onto a 1¼-inch galvanized pipe (be sure to use joint compound). If everything goes according to plan, you will be pumping water within a few hours of when you started! The first flow of water from a newly driven pump is very muddy but will clear up with time and use.

In this chapter we have discussed several different options for "off-grid" water in the event your normal supply runs dry. The caveat to almost all this water is that it likely needs to be filtered to be made safe to drink. The next chapter will discuss the importance of having a reliable water filter on hand.

FOOD

WATER

HEATING

SANITATION

CHAPTER 9

Water Filters

You might be surprised to learn what is in your tap water. For example, in Indianapolis (the capital of Indiana, where I live) there are over ten contaminants in the tap water that exceed the Environmental Working Group's health guidelines, including arsenic, chloroform, nitrate, and radium. Almost all these contaminants are cancer-causing. Some result from the water-purifying process itself, while others make their way into the water through agriculture and farming runoff. Either way, the number of harmful contaminants that exist in the average American's water that is deemed *safe* to drink can be unsettling.

With this in mind, you can see the importance of having an effective water filter in place when you might have to tap in to one or more of the backup water sources described in Chapter 8. This chapter will outline what I believe to be the only three water filtration systems you need to consider for your water preparedness strategy.

Short-Term versus Long-Term Contaminants

Long-term contaminants are water pollutants that will not necessarily kill you right away. I consider plastics to be a long-term water contaminant, as well as pharmaceuticals, pesticides, herbicides, heavy metals, and other chemicals.

Short-term contaminants, on the other hand, are things that can kill you right now. These mainly include biological threats such as giardia, cryptosporidium, hepatitis A, cholera, *E. coli*, and other microbiological organisms. Many of these "live" critters can cause severe vomiting or diarrhea, which can lead to illness, suffering, and even death in a bug-in survival scenario if untreated.

WHAT'S IN YOUR TAP WATER?

Want to read something unsettling? Go to EWG.org/tapwater and type in your zip code to find out what's in your municipal drinking water.

SHOULD YOU FOCUS ON LONG-TERM OR SHORT-TERM CONTAMINANTS?

The answer is both. You should be making a concerted effort to remove *all* of these contaminants from your water *all* of the time, not just during a disaster scenario. The technology exists to do so and (at least in North America) is accessible, affordable, and simple to implement. (Note: Like most important survival tools and supplies, these will likely *not* be available when you need them if you do not already have them when disaster strikes.)

An added benefit of making a concerted effort to clean up your daily drinking water is that not all that much changes if a shelter-in-place survival scenario happens. The process of filtering and drinking water, at least, remains business as usual.

The Big Berkey Water Filter

The Big Berkey water filter is the system I use in my own home daily. It is technically certified as a water purifier, not just a water filter, because it removes 99.9999 percent of pathogenic bacteria. It is a gravity-fed system that sits on a tabletop and requires no electricity. Water from virtually any source previously discussed is simply poured into the upper chamber, allowed to filter through the Black Berkey filters, and comes out the spigot at the bottom safe to drink.

While a Berkey system is available in different sizes, I recommend the 2.5-gallon Big Berkey for most families. This unit will cost you under $300 with two Black Berkey filters. These filters are where all the magic happens, and each one will filter 3,000 gallons of water. As you can see on their website (BerkeyFilters.com/pages/filtration-specifications), Black Berkey filters remove a mind-blowing number of contaminants. Whether it is questionable water from a well, the

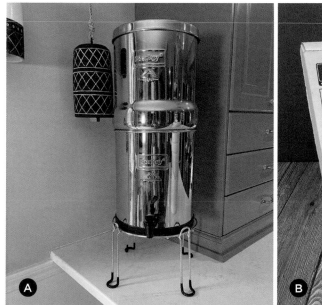

(A) I keep a Big Berkey stainless steel water filter on my kitchen counter. We use this filter every day to filter water for drinking, making coffee, making tea, cooking, and more. (B) The Big Berkey uses two of these Black Berkey carbon filters for gravity filtering out a huge list of contaminants—both short term and long term.

MAKE YOUR OWN WATER FILTER SYSTEM

If you are on a super tight budget but still want the effectiveness of the Black Berkey filters, you can improvise a similar filter system using two 5-gallon plastic buckets instead of the Big Berkey, a spigot bought online, and two Black Berkey filters that cost $120 for the pair. I have included a full step-by-step video for how to do this at the online resource page for this book.

This improvised Big Berkey–style water filter system was made from two 5-gallon buckets and two Black Berkey filters.

tap, a pond, your rain barrel, or almost anywhere else, you can be confident in knowing that if you pour it into the top of a Big Berkey, it is going to come out the other side safe to drink.

A popular question I get about the Big Berkey is when to change the filters. A system with two Black Berkey filters is going to filter 6,000 gallons of water. The easy way to gauge how long they will last is to track how much water you run through the filter for a couple of weeks. Once you determine your daily usage in gallons, you can simple divide 6,000 by that number to determine the approximate number of days they will last. For example, if your family runs 5 gallons of water per day through your Big Berkey, the filters will last 6,000 / 5 = 1,200 days. That is over three years!

In our home, we filter all our drinking and cooking water through our Big Berkey, including any water from plastic bottles to eliminate microplastics. This is a system that you can use every day to improve the quality of one of the most important things you put in your body. And you can use the same system during a disaster, the exact same way, to make sure any backup water you may have to source is 100 percent safe to drink or use for cooking. I have filmed a video about my Big Berkey water filter if you would like to see it. You can find the link at the online resource page for this book.

Here are some pros and cons for the Big Berkey water filter system:

Pros
- Simple operation
- Gravity fed (requires no water pressure or electricity)
- 3,000-gallon carbon filter life (6,000 for two filters)
- Inexpensive, considering how long the filters last
- Convenient tabletop operation
- "Water purifier" level of filtration

Cons
- Not very portable (although they do make some smaller models that are easier to transport)

The Sawyer PointOne Bucket Filter

Although I use the Big Berkey water filter at home, I use the Sawyer PointOne bucket filter system for all my backcountry training events. Sawyer water filters are the leaders in hiking, camping, and backcountry portable water filters. I keep the ultra-portable Sawyer Squeeze in my bug out bag to filter any water I may need to source

I keep a Sawyer Squeeze water filter system in my bug out bag. It is about the size of a roll of quarters and weighs only a few ounces.

(A) Sawyer makes an adapter kit that allows you to turn the Sawyer Squeeze into a larger tabletop gravity-fed system. This is a perfect option for using alternative water sources when sheltering in place at home. (B) The backflushing syringe provided by Sawyer can be used to restore up to 98.5 percent of your Sawyer filter's flow rate.

on-the-go from creeks, ponds, or puddles. You can read about their filters on their website (Sawyer.com/product-categories/water-filtration).

Sawyer filters are primarily biological filters. This means they will cover you for the short-term biological threats that I mentioned previously, but not necessarily some of the long-term chemicals that are so prevalent with industry and agricultural runoff. If biological threats are your main concern and you like the option of a more portable filter system, then a Sawyer filter might be the best option for you. Sawyer also makes a PointZeroTwo model that will filter out viruses as well.

For a more permanent long-term setup like you would want to use during a shelter-in-place scenario, Sawyer offers a bucket adapter kit for $15 (all product links at the resource page for this book) that I really love. This allows you to take their $30 Sawyer Squeeze and turn it into a much larger tabletop gravity-fed filter for easy everyday use. This is the same system I use to filter water during my backcountry survival training events, where I filter wild water for thirty-plus students over the course of several days. For around $50 you can have a large-scale backup filter system that can keep you in safe drinking water for as long as you need.

One clever feature of the Sawyer line of filters is that they include a backflushing syringe that restores up to 98.5 percent of the filter's flow rate. This means that a Sawyer system can be used almost indefinitely without ever having to replace a filter.

Here are some pros and cons of the Sawyer PointOne bucket filter system:

Pros
- Inexpensive ($50 or less for total system)
- Gravity fed (requires no water pressure or electricity)
- 99.99999 percent effective for eliminating biological threats (excluding viruses, although a PointZeroTwo filter can be used to filter out viruses)
- Extremely easy to use and set up
- Unit can be backflushed for nearly indefinite use without having to purchase new filters
- Very portable

Cons
- Filters primarily biological threats

Reverse Osmosis System

While a reverse osmosis system is not my first choice of water filter for disaster preparedness, it certainly deserves a mention. It is often touted as the ultimate form of home water filtration. But whether it is or not takes second place to its lack of simplicity, which is critical in disaster preparedness.

Reverse osmosis is the process of using water pressure to filter water through a semipermeable membrane, and often a pre- and post-carbon filter. It is a common under-the-kitchen-sink mounted system to provide instant filtered water for drinking and often uses a separate smaller faucet that mounts beside the regular one. According to the

CDC (CDC.gov/healthywater/drinking/home-water-treatment/household_water_treatment.html), reverse osmosis systems have a very high effectiveness in removing protozoa (cryptosporidium, giardia), bacteria (*Campylobacter*, *Salmonella*, *Shigella*, *E. coli*), viruses (enteric, hepatitis A, norovirus, rotavirus), and common chemical contaminants such as sodium, chloride, copper, chromium, lead, arsenic, fluoride, radium, sulfate, calcium, magnesium, potassium, nitrate, and phosphorous.

Reverse osmosis is used extensively by the US military to desalinate sea water, as well as filter other sources. But it is important to note that all my research indicates that the military also uses other means of purification, including ultraviolet light and chlorination, in conjunction with reverse osmosis, which suggests a need to kill biologicals that may pass through the membranes.

While reverse osmosis is highly effective at removing many of the threats you will be concerned about when preparing disaster water for drinking, the big drawback is that it requires water pressure to force the water through the series of filters. This is fine if your pressurized city water is still flowing or if you have a means of keeping your well water pressure tank pressurized, but it becomes a deal breaker if not. No water pressure means no reverse osmosis.

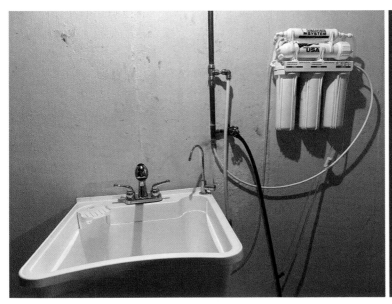

I installed this reverse osmosis water filter system in my basement as an optional disaster preparedness water filtering option.

While it is very convenient to have an in-line effective water filter at your kitchen sink, this system seems more like a luxury for "normal" times rather than a mainstay for disaster preparedness. Here are some pros and cons of the reverse osmosis system:

Pros
- Very effective at removing many contaminants, including biologicals
- Convenient in-line water filter

Cons
- Costs $300–$1,200 depending on the brand and whether you need help installing it
- Must have water pressure to function properly
- Must change out rather expensive cartridges
- Not portable
- Requires routine maintenance
- Complicated multistage filter system with pressure tank and many fittings

Unlike many categories of long-term preparedness, checking off the water filtration box is rather painless. For less than a few hundred dollars and very little effort or skill, you can have nearly 100 percent confidence that you will be able to keep you and your family in clean drinking water. I wish all areas of disaster preparedness were so simple.

CHAPTER 10

Off-Grid Cooking and Boiling

FOOD

WATER

HEATING

SANITATION

This chapter will present several options, varying in price and complexity, for making sure you have a functional off-grid kitchen when you need it most. I have personal experience implementing, building, and installing every idea in this chapter. Just one generation ago, cooking with some of the setups in this chapter was common knowledge. Millions of people around the globe still cook on improvised rocket stoves, with simple utensils, using scavenged wood and twigs found near their homes. The style of cooking outlined in this chapter, especially when fueled by wood, is far more time-tested than any microwave, gas range, toaster, slow cooker, or modern electric oven ever will be. Who knows, with a little practice, you may learn to prefer cooking off the grid!

Barbecue Grill

Although it's not old technology, I would be remiss to not feature the modern barbecue grill. Whether fueled by propane, natural gas, or charcoal, a grill in the right hands is a one-person kitchen. Its functionality for cooking a variety of meats and vegetables is unrivaled in simplicity. And using one is a process most people are familiar with.

The problem for long-term preparedness is fuel. Most people do not stock months', or even weeks', worth of propane or charcoal for daily grilling (although I do have several preparedness friends who store charcoal in large containers as backup fuel for cooking). Those people who have a grill that is hardwired to natural gas might be a little luckier but are still susceptible to disconnection or other interruptions caused by breakages or unavailable deliveries. Many rural residents have

LEARN HOW TO MAKE YOUR OWN CHARCOAL

As a bonus for buying this book, I am offering you a free download tutorial that teaches you step-by-step how to make your own charcoal in your backyard using found limbs and sticks. It is a fascinating process that could come in handy in a long-term bug-in scenario. To download this free PDF, simply visit CreekStewart.com/disaster-charcoal.

I store two extra 20-pound propane tanks in an outside shed. These can be used as backups for the grill or as fuel sources for space heaters (discussed in detail later).

large propane tanks for home heat that are or can be hooked directly to a grill as well. These instances of large on-hand fuel supplies are increasingly becoming the exception and not the norm, especially for those living in the suburbs.

I love the idea of using a barbecue grill as a short-term cooking option. Because of this, I stock two to three 20-pound propane tanks as an extended fuel source. If I grilled using charcoal, I would fill several large garbage cans as a backup. Propane is a fuel that will store for decades without degradation. We will discuss propane as a fuel in more detail later.

Wood-Burning Cookstoves

When it comes to long-term off-grid cooking solutions, the best option is to look to what our not-so-distant ancestors used and what millions of people use every day for cooking: wood. For most people, wood is the most accessible, renewable, and realistic fuel for off-grid disaster cooking. From large split hardwood chunks neatly stacked into cords beside the garage to small handfuls of twigs and pine cones collected in the backyard, there is a use for wood of nearly any size or species in disaster cooking. Following are several options to consider that cover the gamut of cooking stoves, from expensive and prebuilt to improvised and nearly free. Hopefully, one or more of these options will find its way into your long-term preparedness plans.

Before I got married, I lived alone in a small cottage on a river in central Indiana. It was here where I first started cooking on a wood-burning stove. Limited by both space and budget, I purchased and installed a small Jøtul brand Norwegian-made wood stove. Although its design was mainly for heating small spaces, it did have an area on top suitable for cooking and simmering. I almost always had tea brewing and some sort of stew simmering on top of that small stove, even during the warmer summer months.

Wood cookstoves were once a staple appliance in every American kitchen. They served not only as a heating stove for colder months but also as a multifunctional oven, range, hot water heater, and food warmer—all fueled by wood. With a little research, antique cookstoves

(A) My Jøtul freestanding wood stove often had a kettle heating on top. (B) The Fireview by Elmira Stove Works is a beautiful modern wood-burning cookstove. (C) The Milly wood-burning cookstove is made by Italian-based La Nordica.

from years past can be found and restored. But many people do not realize that new wood cookstoves are still in production from several manufacturers in North America, the United Kingdom, and Europe. One of my favorites is the Fireview by Elmira Stove Works (ElmiraStoveWorks.com) in Ontario, Canada. This wood-burning cookstove is as much a piece of art as it is a multifunctional appliance. Its nickel legs, skirt, and Victorian-style decorative trivet hark back to a time when life was slower and, on many levels, simpler. It features a 21-inch firebox, an oven, top and side warmers, and an optional water jacket to supply household hot water.

Another excellent resource for mainly imported wood-burning cookstoves is WoodCookStove.com. They stock several European models and offer free shipping throughout North America. One stove, called Milly, is made by Italian-based La Nordica. This wood-burning cooker features double glass fire doors, a large enameled oven, top cooking plate and rings in polished cast iron, and a top food warmer. What more could you ask for from an off-grid cooking option?

WORTH THE INVESTMENT

The price of a wood-burning cookstove can range from $1,500 to $5,000 and even beyond. It is certainly a commitment of both money and space in your kitchen. But you will be hard-pressed to find a group of people more passionate about something than those who have a wood-burning cookstove. There is something truly magical about cooking and baking using a well-made cookstove.

Ohio-based Lehman's (Lehmans.com) also boasts an impressive selection of wood-burning cookstoves, both online and at their brick-and-mortar location in Kidron, Ohio. Some of the brands they carry include Pioneer Princess, Vermont Bun Baker, and Baker's Choice.

There are few, if any, preparedness purchases as multifunctional and time-tested as the wood-burning cookstove. The ability to cook, bake, warm food, heat water, make coffee, and heat your home—all with one appliance that just burns wood—is extremely appealing to those who wish to be prepared for anything.

EcoZoom Rocket Stove

I realize that integrating a wood-burning cookstove into the average suburban North American kitchen is a big stretch and beyond the scope for most people. However, many preparedness-minded families understand the need for an off-grid cooking and boiling solution. The truth is that millions of people around the world cook meals every day on wood- and charcoal-fueled stoves. Many of these people use some version of a design called a "rocket stove."

Rocket stoves are very efficient cooking stoves that consist of a combustion area and an insulated chimney. They commonly use small-diameter or scavenged wood, which is available to almost anyone, even in large cities. Because of the unique design, rocket stoves produce extremely high heat and almost no smoke. They also produce extraordinarily little mess and turn wood fuel into nothing but a few spoonfuls of white ash. Because of all these advantages, I would encourage you to consider a rocket stove of some type as a backup off-grid cooking solution.

Many different brands and styles of rocket stoves are available for purchase, and I have used most of them. For camping and hiking I use a small one called a Solo Stove; I've included a link to it at the online resource page for this book. But when it comes to a larger at-home solution, I prefer the EcoZoom stove.

The EcoZoom stove is small enough to be portable and stores well in the garage or shed. It is also large enough to be a legit off-grid cooking stove for an entire family, and you don't have to live in a forest full of wood or even own a chainsaw. According to EcoZoom's website (EcoZoom.com), their stoves save up to 70 percent on fuel usage compared to an open fire or inefficient stove and produce 60 percent less smoke. Just a handful of sticks from the backyard or local park is enough fuel to cook an entire meal.

ALTERNATIVES TO WOOD

Besides sticks, you can burn any other type of biomass, such as dried piles of cow dung (seriously, you can).

Some of the easiest meals to make are simple stir-fries of vegetables, beans, rice, and a little meat. There is no better pan for the job than a round-bottom wok to do this. One feature I really like about the EcoZoom stove is that the top burner can accommodate both round-bottom and flat-bottom pans. It is very awkward to

Here I am stir-frying vegetables in a wok on my EcoZoom rocket stove.

The EcoZoom stove operates on small-diameter sticks and twigs that feed into the side fuel chamber while the stove is in use.

cook over most stoves with a wok, but it is a breeze with the EcoZoom. If you are looking for an inexpensive (around $120 online) backup cooking stove that is not dependent on gas, propane, or any other grid-tied fuel, I would encourage you to look at this stove. Mine has served me well over the years in times of recreation and necessity.

Twenty-Five-Brick Rocket Stove

Maybe you like the idea of a rocket stove but are not ready to spend $120 on a backup to store down in the basement for a "just in case" scenario. The solution for you might be a twenty-five-brick rocket stove, an almost-free solution that is perfect for the DIY prepper.

First, hop on your local *Facebook Marketplace* or *craigslist* and find someone giving away a pile of old bricks. Tell them you need twenty-eight or so. You only need twenty-five for this project, but it is always a good idea to have a couple extra.

Then take a brick chisel or brick hammer and split a brick in half (wear safety glasses). If you see any half pieces when you pick up your free bricks be sure to get them, and you can save yourself this step. You will need two half brick pieces and twenty-four full bricks to build your twenty-five-brick rocket stove.

STEP 1

STEP 2

STEP 3

Placing Bricks in a U Shape

On a solid, noncombustible surface, such as dirt, gravel, or stone, place a layer of bricks in a U shape. Use one of the half-brick pieces in one of the corners, as shown.

STEP 2

Placing the Metal Grate on the Bricks

Place a metal grate on top of the U-shaped brick layer. You can buy cheap metal grates at the dollar store or find something else that will work. It does not have to be fancy, but it does need to allow airflow.

STEP 3

Placing Bricks in a U Shape on the Metal Grate

Build a second U-shaped layer on top of the metal grate. Use the second piece of half-brick for this layer. At this point you will have used seven bricks—six full and two halves. The bottom two layers and grate make up the fuel feeding and combustion chamber. The grate serves as a platform for wooden sticks and allows airflow to be pulled from under the fuel and into the chimney above.

STEP 4

STEP 5

STEP 6

STEP 4

Placing Four Bricks on Top of the U Shape

Now stack a four-square of bricks as the next layer. Eleven bricks total will have been used at this point.

STEP 5

Placing Three More Layers of Four Bricks Each

Stack three more four-square layers of brick. These layers will build the chimney, which draws in fresh air through the fuel chamber to flush the fire with oxygen. It is this effect that creates a very efficient and hot fire. Twenty-three bricks will have been used when the chimney is complete.

STEP 6

Building a Fire

To start the fire, loosely pack the chimney with small, dry sticks and twigs. Then, fill the fuel chamber on top of the grate with tinder material such as dry leaves, grass, or pine needles. It's fine if bits of leaves and twigs fall through the grate, as can be seen in the photo, but you do not want to pack underneath the grate with fuel because it will reduce air flow, which is critical to this design. When you light the tinder in the fuel chamber, the heat will rise. As it does, it will pull in fresh air from under the tinder and provide oxygen to the fire. More oxygen will help the fire burn hotter, which will cause the air to rise faster, thus pulling in more fresh oxygen. Once the fire is going well, you will feed the fire with sticks

STEP 7

through the fuel chamber. You put sticks in the chimney only at the beginning to get the fire going.

STEP 7

Cooking on the Brick Stove

Place the last two of the twenty-five bricks on either side of the chimney opening. This gives you a raised platform to place a pot for cooking. If you like, you can place another supporting grate on top of these bricks and put the pot on that.

You now have the knowledge to build an incredibly efficient off-grid rocket stove in under 15 minutes using twenty-five free bricks and a spare metal grate. But what is even more amazing is that it can be powered using scavenged sticks and twigs from just about anywhere.

Double-Burner Cinder Block Rocket Stove

There are an infinite number of rocket stove configurations that can be made using bricks, rocks, blocks, and pavers. This particular design is a unique solution for those who need double burners for larger families or who want to simultaneously cook two different food items at two different temperatures. The rocket stove principle is the same as described for the twenty-five-brick rocket stove, except that this configuration gives you two fuel chambers, two chimneys, and two burners. All the materials for this build can easily be purchased from your local home improvement center for just a few dollars. With a little effort, you might even be able to find them for free somewhere.

STEP 1

STEP 2

STEP 3

STEP 1

Placing the First Cinder Block

Start by placing a standard rectangular 16 × 8 × 8-inch concrete cinder block solid-side up on a flat, noncombustible surface.

STEP 2

Placing Two More Cinder Blocks

Now, place two more cinder blocks vertically on either side. Make sure the cutouts of the vertical blocks face toward the middle block, as shown, and not front to back.

STEP 3

Placing Two Concrete Pavers

In the middle of the two vertical cinder blocks, place two 16 × 8 × 2-inch concrete pavers, as shown. These create the walls of the fuel feeding chambers and the lower portion of the two chimneys.

STEP 4

Inserting a Brick in the Middle

Place a standard brick in the middle of the concrete pavers to divide the channel into two equal-sized chimneys.

STEP 5

Placing the Last Cinder Block on Top

Finally, place a fourth concrete cinder block on top of the lower chimney chambers, cutout-side up, as shown. This block forms the rest of the two chimneys.

STEP 6

Building a Fire

Now each separate chimney and fuel chamber can be loaded with fuel for lighting exactly as described, with the twenty-five-brick rocket stove above. The lower cell of the cinder block on each side provides a perfect storage area for backup fuel that can be fed into the fuel chamber just above it.

Cooking on the Rocket Stove

As you can see in the photo, this setup allows two different burners to be used for cooking. In this case I have water boiling from a tripod on one side and a meal warming in a pot on the other, on top of a metal grate. The two sides of this rocket stove can be fed with different types and amounts of fuel to create different temperatures for cooking.

STEP 7

Kelly Kettle

When it comes to boiling water off the grid, I do not think there is a faster and more efficient stove than the Kelly Kettle. This unique boiler was developed by an Irish fisherman in West Ireland in the late 1800s and is still a family-run business today. The Kelly Kettle is famous for its ability to brew a hot drink or soup amid an Irish storm using a handful of sticks and dried grass from the shoreline.

The small, lightweight stainless steel Kelly Kettle solves an especially important problem for the preparedness-minded family. It boils water in just minutes, completely off-grid, with an astonishingly small amount of wood fuel. The design of the kettle is ingenious. It is like a rocket stove in that it has an insulated chimney with a fuel chamber at the bottom. However, the chimney also serves as a water reservoir—it is hollow all the way around and can be filled with water. The heat and flames that fill the chimney bring the surrounding water to a boil

(A) The stainless steel Kelly Kettle is available with a number of accessories.
(B) The large chimney of the Kelly Kettle is filled with water to boil, and the top is fitted with a pot support for warming soup or cooking a meal at the same time. (Notice the small fuel pieces it requires to operate.)

THE KELLY KETTLE

To see a video of me and my son using the Kelly Kettle to prepare a freeze-dried meal from our long-term food storage pantry, visit the online resource page and look under the Chapter 10 heading.

at breakneck speed. The kettle has a spout near the top, which makes pouring the boiling water into a dehydrated meal pouch or cup extremely easy.

There are several models of the Kelly Kettle. I have the Scout model with a few extras that convert the system into a small grill. Although the cooking portion of this setup is geared more toward small-scale hiking and camping, I believe the water boiler is an interesting addition to the prepper's long-term food pantry. My Kelly Kettle kit includes the following items:

- Large (41-ounce) stainless steel Scout Kelly Kettle
- Large stainless steel cook set, which includes a 32-ounce pot, lid/frying pan, grill set, and pot gripper
- Large stainless steel Kelly Kettle Hobo stove
- Two stainless steel packable Kelly Kettle camping cups with CooLip protectors and measurements inside in both ounces and milliliters
- Two packable stainless steel plates/bowls and Kelly Kettle carrying bag

Open-Fire Cooking

Preparing meals over an open fire is a lost art but should absolutely be a consideration for anyone preparing to cook meals off-grid. All you need is a backyard firepit and a plentiful supply of wood to burn. Unlike rocket stoves that can operate efficiently on smaller sticks and twigs, open-campfire cooking consumes large amounts of wood for almost every meal. Hardwoods such as maple, ash, oak, and hickory are best. Open-fire cooking is best done over hot coals, and the formula for a good hot coal bed is lots of wood and lots of time.

Cooking meals over an open fire is a skill that requires practice and experience, but there is a list of open-fire-specific cooking implements that make mealtime around the firepit much more practical and enjoyable. In most instances, open-fire cooking requires a specific set of cookware and tools. I will elaborate on these in this section. An updated list of links to each item mentioned can be found at the resource page for this book.

ADJUSTABLE GRAVITY GRILL

An adjustable grill is an absolute must for open-fire cooking. This piece of equipment allows for grilling meats and vegetables but also provides a platform for various pots, pans, and kettles. The adjustable feature is a necessity because the heat from an open fire is ever-changing based on wood used, outside temperature, and even wind speed and direction.

An adjustable grill can be set high for cooking over flames or low for steady heat over a hot coal bed.

CAST IRON DUTCH OVEN

Cast iron Dutch ovens are an open-fire cooking staple. These thick and durable ovens are specifically designed with legs and deep-dish lids to be surrounded top and bottom with hot, chunky coals. From cowboy beans to campfire cornbread, the number of off-grid meals that can be prepared in a Dutch oven is mind-boggling. Conveniently, many of the simple foods that store well in long-term food storage are also very well suited for Dutch oven cooking: Beans, rice, cornmeal, freeze-dried meals, lentils, oatmeal, split peas, and many other dry goods make fantastic Dutch oven meals. A lid stand and lid-lifter are two especially useful accessories when cooking in a Dutch oven over an open fire.

CAST IRON COOKWARE

Cast iron pots and pans are the go-to cookware of choice for the rigors of open-fire cooking. Not only are they virtually indestructible, but they also hold up to pretty much any cooking circumstance. Whether

This cast iron Dutch oven is buried in the coals of a fire. Notice the deep-dish lid that holds hot coals on top for even cooking all around.

Two Dutch oven accessories: A lid stand (left) provides a clean spot to put your lid while checking on the food inside, and a lid-lifter (right) is designed to safely lift the piping-hot lid from a Dutch oven.

over an open flame or sitting right on the hot coals, cast iron can handle the heat. In an off-grid scenario, the last thing you want to worry about is babying your cookware. While cast iron cookware is ideal for sheltering-in-place, it is far too heavy and bulky to carry in a backpack or for bugging out. More portable options include those made from aluminum and titanium.

When it comes to shopping for cast iron cookware, there are many brands to choose from. The two brands I have experience with are Lodge and Camp Chef. I have had great success over the fire and in the home oven with both. I always keep an eye out at yard sales and flea markets for cast iron cookware as well. Cast iron begins to rust and look awful if not maintained and oiled regularly. People often assume their pans are ruined because of rust, but they are wrong. Cast iron can be beautifully restored and reseasoned with a little elbow grease and cooking oil. I have purchased rusty cast iron skillets at yard sales for a few dollars that are easily worth $80 or more after restoration.

Cast iron skillets come in many different shapes and sizes.

Besides a couple of good skillets in different sizes, one cast iron piece to seriously consider is a reversible grill and griddle. I use my Lodge brand version of this more than I ever thought I would. The grill is ideal for grilling meats and vegetables, and the griddle is perfect for pancakes, tortillas, and scrambled eggs.

One of the biggest tips I can give you when cooking over an open fire with cast iron is to preheat your skillet. Preheating helps release the infused nonstick qualities of the pan. I always place my pan near the heat at least 15 minutes before I am ready to cook. When it comes time for cleanup, a well-seasoned piece of cast iron cookware should not be difficult to clean. Always clean when that pan is hot, right after cooking. Scrub with a stiff, nonmetal brush to get off all the food bits and then wipe dry. Soap is optional. Don't be too concerned with

RESTORING CAST IRON

I have included a free video at the online resource page for this book if you would like to learn my process for restoring and reseasoning cast iron cookware.

Here I'm cooking almond flour flatbread and mini hot dogs on a Lodge brand cast iron griddle.

removing all the cooking oil or grease. Residual oil will help prevent the pan from rusting and keep that nonstick seasoning in place.

Off-grid cooking is a step back in time and requires more practice, patience, and skill than are needed for many modern instant meals that come from a bag, can, or freezer package. That, however, is a small price to pay for the flexibility to prepare meals even when electricity, propane, natural gas, and even solar energy are unavailable.

HEATING AND SANITATION

This book exists to help you cross off the most important categories in long-term preparedness. I've focused on the areas that make the biggest difference when disaster strikes. You are already working on food and water. These final chapters will cover several other vital preps, including off-grid heating and sanitation.

Regulating core body temperature is one of our most immediate survival threats. I will help you choose and implement an off-grid heating solution for your home. Next, I will show you how to build an off-grid composting toilet to deal with human waste in the event your bathroom becomes defunct and the toilet stops flushing. Diseases caused from the misappropriation of human waste are a huge concern in a disaster scenario. I will make sure you are all set in the sanitation department to round out your big dominos.

FOOD

WATER

HEATING

SANITATION

CHAPTER 11

Off-Grid Heating

This chapter is especially important if you live in a four-season environment. Recent history has shown us that stints of unusually cold weather can have devastating effects, especially in areas that would not normally expect it. Not being able to heat your home in cold weather is not just about staying warm. It causes a cumulative effect of chaos that affects almost every aspect of human survival. If you do not have an off-grid solution for at least temporary backup heat, then you need one. This chapter will outline options for you to consider and implement.

You will notice that several of the alternative heat options mentioned in this chapter are remarkably simple, requiring very little commitment or money. It was my goal to offer up practical solutions for the average suburban household. I know from experience that the more trouble and commitment a backup plan requires, the less likely people will be to act on it. I have tried to introduce less complicated and therefore more feasible ideas to increase the chances that people will actually put some of these backup plans into place.

Wood-Burning Stove / Fireplace

Neither sets of my grandparents had an electric furnace or central heat of any kind. Neither of their home heating solutions was tied to a grid, pipe, or wire that went beyond the border of their backyard. Both had completely different types of fuel, and both were always ready for a cold disaster whether they were planning to be or not. One set of grandparents heated with a combination of kerosene space heaters and a centrally located propane fireplace (detailed later in this chapter). The other set heated their two-story home exclusively with one wood-burning fireplace.

There was a time when nearly every American home was heated by some type of wood-burning fireplace or freestanding stove. Slowly, wood heat gave way to some version of coal, oil, gas, or electricity. According to the 2016 census, 38.7 percent of US homes were heated by electricity, 48.1 percent by utility gas, and only 1.9 percent by wood. That means that over 86 percent of homes in 2016 relied on the utility grid for heat. Those are some very scary statistics, and indeed, I have seen countless friends and family members over the years transition their wood-burning fireplace into a grid-tied natural gas or propane insert. Burning wood is not the easiest way to stay warm, and the allure of a simple, cleaner-burning remote-control fireplace has lulled many into an easier but less independent way of life.

For the preparedness-minded person, the addition of a wood-burning fireplace or stove can provide a renewable source of heat, assuming a reliable source of wood is available. If you live in a home where an original wood-burning stove or fireplace has been fitted with a gas-burning alternative, it may be worth considering the possibility of switching back. It will likely require a chimney inspection, but, in general, it is a painless and inexpensive project. You might be able to use the existing gas line as a gas log lighter for igniting your wood logs, which is a nice convenience. Unfortunately, if the original fireplace is a gas-burning one, the project of switching to wood is not so simple. It would likely require an entirely new chimney—if it could even be done at all.

Installing a new wood-burning stove or fireplace in an existing home requires a dedicated space and certain clearances for safety, and even then, some homes simply cannot be fitted with one. You can expect to spend at least $2,000 and up for the job. If you do not

The wood-burning fireplace at my training facility in Indiana easily heats up to 2,000 square feet of indoor cafeteria, kitchen, and bunk rooms. Notice the mounted pot hanger for open-fire cooking as well.

have wood available on your property and do not know someone who does, firewood delivery is always an option. A little research in your local classifieds will likely present a few ambitious woodcutters who will deliver split and seasoned firewood to your doorstep. I have found that many tree trimming companies are happy to get rid of the wood they cut for much less than someone who cuts and sells wood

A WOOD VEE

Stacking wood can be messy. A big pile of wood is a safe haven for insects, mice, and other critters. One solution I like for the wood I stack near my firepit and patio areas is called a wood vee, and you can make one in about 5 minutes with just two cinder blocks and four 2 × 4-inch boards. Be sure to place the boards as shown, with the short sides facing up and down. (If you place them the other way, with the long flat sides facing up and down, the boards will bend and break under the weight.) Also make sure the cinder blocks are positioned on a solid, flat surface so your structure does not tip over. A wood vee minimizes the amount of wood touching the ground and makes for a much cleaner woodpile overall. As I use up wood from my wood vee, I replenish it from a larger woodpile.

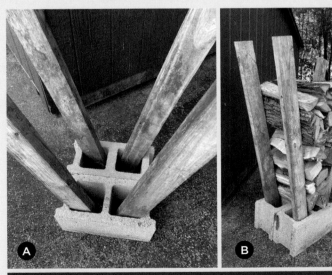

(A) This wood vee is assembled and ready for wood. (B) A wood vee is loaded with split wood.

for a living—sometimes they will give it to you just for hauling it off. *Facebook Marketplace* is loaded with listings of people trying to give away wood or dead trees in exchange for simply cutting them up and hauling them off. Online sources can be a fantastic source of wood if you live in the city or suburbs and do not have land of your own. The importance of planning in advance cannot be overemphasized. Whether it's wood, or any other survival resource, if you wait until you and everyone else needs it at the same time, it will not be available. The only preparations that matter are the ones you make before a disaster strikes.

Cutting and splitting wood yourself requires a few tools of the trade. A gas-powered chainsaw and hydraulic wood splitter are modern necessities. But, of course, those require fuel. If you are forced to

Having manual woodcutting and splitting tools on hand could make the difference between having a fire or not.

My wife and I tested our used crosscut saw on some fallen timber in our back woods.

shelter in place for an uncertain period, access to fuel may be interrupted. This would limit your use of these items to your on-hand fuel storage, which opens a whole new can of worms to think about. Human-powered alternatives used by the old-timers include a few handsaws, a good axe, a splitting maul, and a handful of steel splitting wedges. I purchased a used two-person manual crosscut saw to have on hand just in case. A heavy-duty wagon to transport split wood is a good idea as well.

WOOD TRUTHS

There is an adage about wood that is certainly true: Wood warms you thrice: once when you cut it, once when you split it, and once when you burn it.

You can estimate needing roughly three cords of split and seasoned wood to heat around 1,000 square feet of space for an entire cold-weather season. A cord of wood is 4 feet tall by 4 feet wide by 8 feet long. Three of those is a lot of wood—and a lot of work. Just to give you a hauling image, my small 1986 Ford Ranger pickup truck will hold about a half cord of wood in its bed.

Many people will tell you that burning wood as your main source of heat is a lifestyle choice. I would agree. I personally love the comfort of a wood-burning fireplace or stove, but gathering wood is at minimum a part-time job. I will also tell you that combining the use of a wood stove with other heating options during times of normalcy takes the pressure off having to source as much wood, but gives you the option of backup heat if you ever needed to depend on it. The bonus is you can relax and read a book by the fire. There is truly no substitute for that.

Kerosene Space Heaters

As I mentioned earlier, one set of my grandparents relied heavily on kerosene space heaters to warm their home throughout winter. Each fall they had enough kerosene delivered to get them through several months of regular use. You can expect kerosene to store well for up to five years, which makes it an ideal preparedness storage fuel if you use it on a regular basis.

Kerosene is made from crude oil and is similar to heating oil and diesel fuel, except it burns cleaner and doesn't gel in cold temperatures. It is considered a safe fuel because its flash point is around 100°F. In comparison, the flash point of gasoline is around −45°F, so it is therefore much more volatile. In fact, you can throw a lit match onto a puddle of kerosene and it will not ignite. Kerosene also remains viscous across a wide range of temperatures, which makes it an ideal fuel for outside storage, unlike heating oil, which tends to gel up in cold temperatures. For this reason, kerosene is a popular heating oil in the Northeast, where temperatures get very cold.

KEROSENE DELIVERY

Kerosene is a common fuel for residential delivery, and a quick Google search for "kerosene delivery and YOUR CITY, STATE" will list local suppliers. The website FuelWonk.com is a great place to find local suppliers as well.

Kerosene can be burned as a lamp oil if necessary. However, lamp oil burns cleaner and with less fumes because it goes through additional stages of purification. Proper ventilation is ideal when using kerosene as lamp oil, but being able to use it for lighting in a grid-down scenario in a pinch is a bonus. Having a couple of oil-powered hurricane lamps on hand for this purpose is always a good idea when the power is out. Oil lamps burn roughly ½ an ounce of oil per hour.

This means that 1 gallon of kerosene or lamp oil will create light for over 500 hours. That makes stocking both a no-brainer.

The kerosene heater I have as a backup space heater is from my local home improvement center; it cost less than $150. It heats around 1,000 square feet and runs for 8–12 hours on the 2-gallon kerosene fuel tank—all without any electricity. It has two batteries that create a spark for ignition, but even that process can be done with a match. This is a similar unit to what my grandparents used to heat their home throughout my entire childhood. I use it each winter while working in my garage, and it warms up the two-car garage in less than 15 minutes.

With two steel drums of kerosene and a manual fuel pump in my shed, I can keep my home somewhat comfortable and keep my pipes from freezing for roughly thirty straight days in very cold temperatures

(A) Kerosene can be bulk delivered to your home and stored in large tanks or 55-gallon metal drums. It can also be purchased in smaller containers like this one I bought at a local home improvement center. (B) I keep a kerosene space heater as a part of my long-term preparedness strategy. I also use this heater to warm up my garage when working on projects in the winter. It burns clean and is safe for indoor use (with caution).

with no other heat source at all besides my little $150 space heater. In Indiana, that is almost half of our coldest winter season.

KEROSENE CAVEATS

Heating with kerosene does not come without inherent dangers. First, kerosene heaters are fire hazards. Many homes have been burned to the ground because of them. You must follow the manufacturer's safety directions to the letter for ignition and make sure the heater has clearance from anything flammable. The surfaces of kerosene heaters can also get extremely hot, so be especially careful when using them around kids.

Kerosene is not the cleanest-burning fuel on the market. Burning it produces a distinct odor and carbon monoxide. Although kerosene heaters are approved for use indoors, it is a good idea to allow for proper ventilation. Typically, a couple of cracked windows nearby will do the job. Never use kerosene heaters in an enclosed small bedroom.

In general, a kerosene space heater is an extremely easy and stress-free backup home heating solution. While this heater is not technically grid-tied, you are dependent on a reliable source of fuel for it to be used as a long-term solution. But for short-term intermittent use, it is hard to beat the advantages of having one (and some fuel) in storage just in case.

KEROSENE COOKSTOVES

During the late 1800s and early 1900s, before electricity gained popularity, kerosene cookstoves and ranges were immensely popular in American kitchens. They were a cleaner and quicker alternative to the ubiquitous wood-burning cookstove. Antique kerosene cookstoves in various sizes can still be found for sale on the Internet and may be an interesting backup cooking option if you decide that kerosene is a fuel worth storing. One of the most popular brands was called the Perfection Cookstove.

Propane Heaters

Unlike virtually any other fuel, propane will store for decades in a proper tank without degradation. This makes propane an incredibly attractive storage fuel for those interested in long-term preparedness. Millions of Americans currently heat their homes and cook with propane fuel. Especially in rural areas where natural gas is not available, a large pill-shaped propane tank is a common backyard fixture.

My parents currently heat their home exclusively with propane. As they aged, they made the decision to put a propane fireplace insert in their wood-burning fireplace and install a large propane tank behind the garage to feed it. One full tank will provide them with months' worth of heat. Installing or retrofitting an existing fireplace to burn propane is certainly an option for off-grid heat. But if this sounds like a larger project than you are ready for, there are several smaller-scale backup options that are a little less daunting.

A step down from a propane fireplace is a wall-mounted or free-standing ventless propane heater. (Note: These can also use natural gas if you already have natural gas running to your home.) "Ventless"

Large propane tanks like this one can hold hundreds of gallons of propane, which can last for months of use.

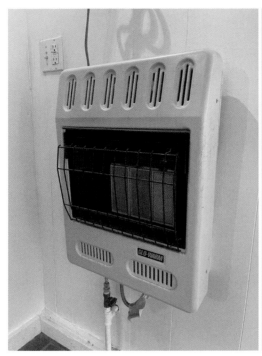

A ventless wall-mounted propane heater like this one is a very economical backup heat source if you have natural gas or propane.

means that you do not have to vent the heater outside, which makes installation a little easier. You can simply ignite it for instant heat after it is hooked up to your outside propane tank. Most ventless propane and natural gas heaters will heat between 500 and 1,000 square feet. These units must be directly tied to a large propane tank or natural gas line, as the typical 20-pound barbecue grill–sized propane tanks are too small for them.

Propane is a common fuel for residential delivery, and a quick Google search for "propane delivery and YOUR CITY, STATE" will list local suppliers. The website FuelWonk.com is a great place to find local suppliers as well. These suppliers are the first to call if you're interested in propane. They will know all the local regulations about installing a propane tank and will be able to walk you through the entire process. Many vendors have tank lease programs as well, which can make getting a propane tank more economical.

If you like the idea of propane but are wanting even less of a commitment, then you may want to consider the Buddy Heater by Mr. Heater. I have owned a Buddy Heater for many years and have used

(A) I've had my Buddy Heater for ten-plus years. Notice the side-mounted 1-pound propane canister. These canisters are available at most camping and outdoor stores. (B) An optional hose and filter make it possible to hook up a Buddy Heater to a 20-pound barbecue grill–sized tank. This is a very easy and inexpensive option for backup heat.

it countless times. Buddy Heaters are made to use 1-pound propane canisters but can also hook up to a 20-pound barbecue grill–sized propane tank with an optional hose and filter. This drastically extends the burn time for at-home heat.

The Buddy Heater costs a little over $100 and is safe to use indoors. It will run for 3–6 hours on a 1-pound canister depending on the heat setting and is stated to heat a 225-square-foot space. If nothing else, this could be a great solution to keep the water pipes from freezing in a vulnerable area of your home.

Whole-House Generators

Small gasoline-powered generators are great for short-term power outages, but unless you are storing large amounts of gasoline, these are not going to provide power for long. Most people I know do not have the means to store large amounts of gasoline, as it typically requires a distant outbuilding and/or above- or below-ground metal tanks. It is common for farmers to have large tanks of fuel on hand, but not so much in the suburbs.

I keep a small gasoline-powered Honda generator on hand for short-term emergencies.

I own a small gasoline generator, but it is not a part of my long-term power plan for electricity or heat. However, whole-house generators powered by natural gas or propane are another story. These are large generators that typically tie directly to your electric box and fire up when the power goes off. Natural gas is much less likely to go off-line than electricity, which happens all the time. With a large propane storage tank, you can feed a whole-house generator for a long time, especially if it is used intermittently. This type of power could be a perfect solution for keeping your electric furnace, blowers, baseboard heat, or space heaters operational.

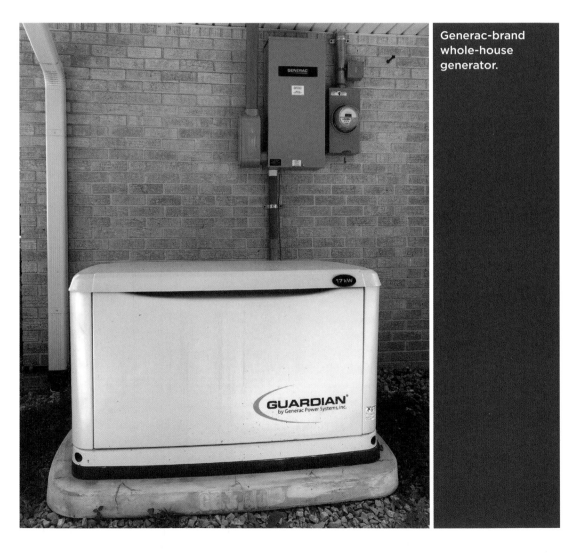

Generac-brand whole-house generator.

Installation of a whole-house generator is a job for a professional. There are local heating specialists in your area who do it all the time. The price is the painful part, as you can expect to pay several thousand dollars by the time you are done. You can also expect to pay a small annual fee for servicing, cleaning, and maintenance to keep it in tip-top shape.

If a whole-house generator seems like something that would be a good solution for you and your home, here are three places to get started:

- Kohler: KohlerPower.com/en/residential/generators
- Genmac: Genmac.it/en
- Generac: Generac.com

Hopefully, one or more of the home heating options I have presented in this chapter will make sense for you, your home, and your family. I have also provided online links to everything mentioned throughout this chapter at the online resource page for this book.

FOOD

WATER

HEATING

SANITATION

CHAPTER 12

Off-Grid Bathroom

How you will use the bathroom during a chaotic long-term disaster could quite possibly be the most important prep you make. The inability to safely deal with human waste can spread disease faster than just about anything out there. The improper handling of human feces has been the bane of civilizations throughout human history. This chapter will teach you how to handle, store, and potentially even reuse both #1 and #2. By the end of this chapter you may even wonder why you have flushing toilets to begin with.

The Problem of Human Sewage

Under normal circumstances, you flush the toilet and everything disappears, never to be seen again, like magic. However, there are countless disasters that could interrupt the regular "flow" of this process. From power outages and floods to earthquakes and water shortages, you have the potential for serious problems if the toilet stops flushing. Luckily, there is an extremely easy and inexpensive solution to this problem, and one that I have proven to be effective in my own household for over eight months straight.

The Composting Sawdust Toilet

Contrary to popular belief, you do not need water to use the bathroom. Nor do you need a conventional toilet, a sewer system, a pump, or a septic tank. All you really need is some sawdust and a plastic bucket. An off-grid toilet is absolutely one thing from this book that

The only materials needed for a very effective off-grid toilet are a 5-gallon bucket, a snap-on bucket toilet seat, and some sawdust.

you should implement by the end of the week. You do not have to use it on a regular basis, but you should have the materials and supplies on hand to deploy it at a moment's notice. You will need only three very inexpensive items:

- 5-gallon plastic bucket
- Toilet seat that snaps onto a 5-gallon bucket (search online for "5-gallon bucket toilet seat" or find the link to the one I suggest at the online resource page for this book)
- Sawdust

Composting is simply a word that means decaying organic matter. Sticks and leaves turn into a form of compost as they decay on the forest floor. This process feeds the living plants and trees. Many gardening enthusiasts use a composting bin to turn leaves, food scraps, and grass clippings into a nutrient-rich fertilizer. Human waste is also an organic material that can be turned into compost. But, by itself, human waste has a tough time composting. It needs to be mixed with other organic matter to provide carbon and other necessary elements. Sawdust is the perfect additive for this. Peat is another popular alternative. The process of assembling and using this composting sawdust toilet is quite simple.

THE DANGERS OF HUMAN WASTE

According to the World Health Organization, life-threatening human pathogens carried by sewage include cholera, typhoid, and dysentery. Other diseases resulting from sewage contamination of water include schistosomiasis, hepatitis A, intestinal nematode infections, and more.

The first step is to snap the toilet lid onto your bucket. Congrats! You have built your toilet. Next, add 1–2 inches of sawdust, peat, or similar material to the bottom of the bucket. Now you are ready to start using the toilet. After going #1, #2, or both right on top of the sawdust below, use a scoop to shovel in a layer of sawdust on top of your waste. It is okay to toss in your used toilet paper too, but nothing else. Toilet paper is an organic composting material as well. Cover everything by about 1 inch of sawdust.

Repeat the process until the bucket is too full for comfort, then replace the toilet seat lid with a solid lid for storage. These full composting buckets can be stacked in a garage or shed, under a deck, in

(A) My son River and I have been using this 5-gallon bucket toilet every day for over eight months. The feed sack is filled with sawdust to add organic composting material to the bucket after each use. (B) Our full composting toilet is sealed and stored under our 305-gallon water tank during the several months' composting process. This emits absolutely zero odor.

the barn, or behind the house. While in storage, bacteria and fungi will do their magic work and turn everything inside into a naturally composted humus-like material. This process normally takes around three months depending on temperatures. The resulting compost can then be dumped into a secondary compost pile in the corner of your yard or used to fertilize your trees or flower beds. Do not use human waste compost in your vegetable garden due to risk of disease transmission.

The idea of a composting toilet is not new. It is a concept that has been used around the globe and throughout history with great success for a very long time. Many off-grid homes use them. However, most people do not realize just how simple and effective they are. While filming my online course about long-term disaster preparedness (OutdoorCore.com/courses/how-to-build-a-long-term-food-storage-pantry-for-bug-in-survival), my son River and I used this same toilet in our garage for over eight months. I was so impressed I told my wife that we should do away with all our flushing toilets. (That is a battle I have yet to win.) But for disaster preparedness, if you have sawdust and buckets, you have a solution for using the bathroom safely, without being tied to the sewer or water grid.

In all honesty, a 5-gallon bucket can be a little tippy, especially if you are a bigger person. The solution is again quite simple. With a little wood and a few screws, you can build a toilet box with a regular toilet seat that sits over a 5-gallon bucket. I did this and made mine the standard 15-inch toilet seat height, which covers the 14.5-inch-high 5-gallon bucket perfectly. I made the box large enough to fit a second bucket of sawdust inside as well. Hinges on the back of the top give easy access to everything inside and keep the contents out of sight when your preparedness friends are over.

The most popular question I get is about the smell. You would imagine that a bucket of sawdust and human waste would stink. It does not. In fact, our composting toilet smells like cedar. Once covered up, the sawdust does an amazing job of trapping any odor associated with #1 or #2. I know it is hard to believe, but it is true. The resulting compost also has absolutely no odor at all, other than that of dirt.

(A) A wooden toilet box fitted with a regular toilet seat is more stable than a 5-gallon bucket. (B) Hidden inside the toilet box is the 5-gallon bucket composting toilet and an extra bucket of sawdust to use for layering.

Sawdust or peat are key ingredients to this process. Without them composting will not happen, and you will just end up with toxic buckets of stinky human sludge. You can buy large bundles of peat at your local gardening center. Or you can do what I did, and find a sawmill that will give you all the sawdust you could ever haul. I keep about ten 50-pound feed sacks full in my garage. A customer in my online preparedness course gets hers from the local high school woodworking class. You can also find free sawdust on *Facebook Marketplace*. Other sources include woodworking stores, cabinet shops, lumberyards, and the woodcutting department at big-box home improvement centers. Most of these places will give it to you for free if you just ask.

The Backyard Latrine

In the event you do not take my advice and acquire the supplies to build a composting toilet, or if you run out of organic material to use in one, every backyard can be turned into an improvised trench latrine. The concept is simple.

Start by digging a long trench that is roughly 10–12 inches deep. Neatly pile the excavated dirt all to one side of the trench. The longer the trench, the more times you will be able to use the bathroom without have to dig again. When it is time to use the bathroom, you will straddle the trench at one end. When finished, use the dirt on the side to cover up your new additions to the trench. With each trip to the trench latrine, you will move farther along the trench until it is completely covered back in. Then, it's time to dig a new trench, and repeat the process.

This backyard trench latrine is dug and ready for use.

I have built many trench latrines for my survival courses while in the backcountry. It is a highly effective way to handle human waste for several people. You want to take special care not to place a trench latrine anywhere near a water source, especially your well. I typically allow for 100 feet from any water source.

A few simple additions can make a backyard trench latrine much more comfortable.

1. A toilet seat chair can be purchased for around $30, or any kind of folding or wooden chair can be modified with minimal effort with a 4-inch grinder or jigsaw.
2. A pop-up booth for privacy is a must if you live in a subdivision. These types of pop-up booths are typically sold as camping shower booths or changing booths, but they make

(A) A folding toilet seat chair is a perfect addition to a trench latrine. (B) A pop-up camp shower booth can provide privacy if you live in a subdivision.

the perfect backyard latrine privacy booth. You can find them for around $30.

3. Of course, this preparedness project is not complete without a stockpile of toilet paper. My advice on that subject is to calculate how much toilet paper your family uses for one week and round up each partially used roll to the nearest whole roll for a one-week total. Use this weekly amount to calculate and store a minimum of three months' worth of toilet paper.

If history tells us anything, soft white paper might become more valuable than green dollars if the grid goes down.

Conclusion

The goal of this book is to help you create a personalized plan for some of the most important home preparedness subjects. Every project I have detailed in this book is important, and you should decide how you will move forward with each one. Here are some final thoughts on how to continue your preparedness planning.

Let Go of Perfection

There is a saying: "Done is better than perfect." Developing the perfect plan often gets in the way of action. It is action, not perfection, that is the key to being prepared for a future disaster. I have been working on my own preparedness plan for over twenty years, and it still feels cobbled together. My challenge to you moving forward is to focus on action instead of perfection.

Start Small

Having read this book, you may feel overwhelmed. The key to action is small, bite-sized chunks. When putting together your disaster-ready home, it does not matter where you start. Just pick one project, make a small decision, and act. The sawdust composting toilet is easy. Get the materials this week and cross it off your list. Then, choose another topic, like water, and make a small decision there. The collection of your many small decisions over time will make a profound impact if and when the grid goes down. Remember, slow and steady wins the race.

Maintain Your Plan

Especially when it comes to storing food and water, it is vital to maintain your plan. This is why it is so important to store what you eat and eat what you store. Rotating your stored food is the key to a practical plan that works long-term. Never buy food that you do not eat on a regular basis unless it is specifically for twenty-plus-year storage (freeze-dried or bulk goods). Following are a few guidelines beyond rotation for maintaining the long-term food storage plan you have put into place.

KEEP A TIMELINE TALLY

Remember when you set your timeline goals at the beginning of the book? Now is the time to mark your progress on meeting those goals. Every time you add/subtract food or water to/from your long-term pantry storage, be sure to update a servings tally on a Timeline Tally Sheet. You can download the one I use at the online resource page for this book. This is imperative for knowing how much you have stored and for how long. Otherwise, it becomes almost impossible to keep track of your stores. I keep track of only four things:

1. Grain servings
2. Protein servings
3. Fruit/vegetable servings
4. Water in gallons

Keeping this tally sheet will allow you to quickly calculate exactly how many servings of these items you have on hand and thus where you measure up on your timeline goals. The tallying process can be a little tedious at first, but it is critical if you want to track your goals. If you do not do this, you will have to repeatedly do a full pantry inventory to count servings.

KEEP A PANTRY SHOPPING LIST

One key to a full long-term pantry is making a note each time you pull something from it for use in the day-to-day kitchen. It is very easy to get into the habit of "shopping" from the long-term pantry and not replenishing. And then it is critical to not only replenish but to add to your stores as well. The best way to do this is to keep a shopping list in your long-term pantry that you add to each time something is removed. I used to keep a notepad, but now my wife and I use a shared app on our phone. Either of us can update the list, and we are not allowed to pull from the pantry unless we update the list. This list is then combined with our regular grocery list. Once your long-term pantry is built to the size you need it for your goal timeline, maintenance becomes very easy as long as you follow this protocol.

BIANNUAL INSPECTION

You should inspect your long-term pantry at least twice a year. Your inspection goal is to head off any issues before they develop. These could include swelling cans, moisture around shelving units, signs of insect or rodent infestations, or anything else that does not look normal. This should also include a general check to make sure you are actually rotating the short-term (less than three years' expiration date) in your long-term food storage pantry.

ANNUAL RAIN BARREL WASH-OUT

Even though rainwater is very clean, dirt and debris still make their way onto your roof and into your gutters. Over time this sediment can collect in your rain barrel. A point should be made each year to spray and wash out your rain barrel. This is easily done with a regular garden hose. If you live in an environment with four seasons, your rain barrel should be disconnected and emptied before temperatures drop below freezing. This is also a great time to wash it out.

FIVE-YEAR WATER STORAGE REFRESH

Every five years you should drain, rinse, and replenish your long-term water storage containers. This can be a time-consuming task and is my least favorite part of preparedness maintenance, but it is important nonetheless. (I spent the first fifteen years doing this every year, so consider yourself lucky!)

ANNUAL NEEDS EVALUATION

It is very important to do an annual needs evaluation. This is a very intentional look at your current circumstances to make any necessary adjustments to your pantry and preparedness plan. Here are some questions to ask in an annual assessment:

- ❏ Are my timeline goals still the same? Am I preparing for a longer or shorter timeline than I had initially set?

- ❏ If my timeline is different, have I set new storage goals in terms of on-hand food servings and gallons of water?

- ❏ Are there any new members of the family to consider with long-term storage? Or fewer family members?

- ❏ Have there been any changes in diets, sensitivities, or medical conditions (for example, gluten-free, diabetes) that affect what should be stored in my long-term food pantry?

- ❏ Are there any new pets that need to be accounted for?

- ❏ Has my location changed in a way that may affect one or more of my renewable water sources?

- ❏ Am I rotating through stored food that has an expiration date of less than three years?

- ❏ Have I implemented any changes learned from live drills (detailed next)?

Live Drills

Putting your preps to the test during mock live drills is without question the best way to maintain and find the hiccups in your plan. Live drills can be as simple or complex as you make them, but using the systems you have put in place builds competency and confidence. Following are a few example live drills to consider:

- **Friday Night Food Storage Dinner:** Rarely do your bulk dry foods such as rice, beans, TVP, or whole-wheat berries fit perfectly into your 5-gallon containers or FoodBricks. There is almost always some left over. No worries—these extras make great practice! One Friday a month, make dinner from food items not in rotation in your long-term food storage pantry. Challenge yourself by learning how to prepare dry bulk goods, or try to liven up freeze-dried meals with fresh herbs or wild game. Make mental notes of what you like and what you don't and implement any pertinent changes.
- **Pull the Plug:** Surprise your family one weekend by turning off the electricity in your home. You will be shocked at how much you learn about your systems in just two days without power.
- **Rocket Stove Cooking:** It is one thing to know how to build a rocket stove from bricks, but it is something entirely different to use one for cooking. Choose a day to cook all meals using only one brick rocket stove.
- **Bucket Weekend:** Designate a weekend when normal toilets are off limits. By simulating a sewage backup or failure, you will find out what you like and do not like about your sawdust composting toilet really quick. Use that information to plan for a time when you might have to use it for much longer.

Live drills are especially important if you have children. The experience of voluntarily trying something as a practice exercise helps reduce anxiety and fear in the event that it needs to be done out of necessity one day. There is no end to the variety of live drills you could come up with. I would love to hear what live drill ideas you have, and what you learn while testing them. Share your updates by emailing me at creek@creekstewart.com.

Online Resources

If you have not already done so, take a minute to visit the online resource page for this book. It is loaded with product links, downloadable resources, training videos, access to online courses about preparedness, and more. It is my hope that this book is just the beginning of our training together.

In light of recent natural disasters, civil unrest, and health crises, I believe it is not a matter of *if* but *when* each of us will need to tap in to the preparations we are making today. I hope I am wrong, but I love my family too much to rely on hope as a plan. I bet you do too. The good news is that hope and action are not mutually exclusive. You can have hope *and* take action. You can be positive *and* plan for bad things. You can do good in the midst of bad times. So, prep on, my friend, with a smile on your face, and hope you never have to tap in to the disaster plans you put in place!

Index

About the Author

Creek Stewart is an expert survival instructor and the author of *Survival Hacks* and the bestselling Build the Perfect Bug Out series of books. Creek has hosted three TV programs on The Weather Channel: *Fat Guys in the Woods*, *SOS: How to Survive*, and *Could You Survive? with Creek Stewart*. Creek has been featured as a guest expert in numerous media outlets, including the *Today* show, *Fox & Friends*, *The Doctors*, *Men's Fitness*, *Backpacker*, and *Outdoor Life*. Creek is the owner and founder of the Willow Haven Outdoor survival training school, located in central Indiana, and APOCABOX, a bimonthly survival subscription box that ships to thousands of loyal subscribers every other month. He is the recipient of the prestigious Outstanding Eagle Scout Award, which is bestowed by the Boy Scouts of America to Eagle Scouts who have demonstrated outstanding achievement at the local, state, or national level. Creek lives in central Indiana with his wife, Sarah, and two children, River and Lakelyn.